SO MANY BABIES

SO MANY BABIES

My Life Balancing a
Busy Medical Career & Motherhood

SUSAN LANDERS, MD

NEW YORK

LONDON • NASHVILLE • MELBOURNE • VANCOUVER

SO MANY BABIES

My Life Balancing a Busy
Medical Career & Motherhood

© 2022 **SUSAN LANDERS, MD**

Published in New York, New York, by Morgan James Publishing. Morgan James is a trademark of Morgan James, LLC. www.MorganJamesPublishing.com

ISBN 978-1-63195-450-4 paperback
ISBN 978-1-63195-451-1 eBook
Library of Congress Control Number: 2020923590

Cover Design by:
Chris Treccani
www.3dogdesign.net

Morgan James is a proud partner of Habitat for Humanity Peninsula and Greater Williamsburg. Partners in building since 2006.

Get involved today! Visit
www.MorganJamesBuilds.com

For David, Anne, and Laura—with my whole heart.

TABLE OF CONTENTS

ACKNOWLEDGMENTS

I am grateful to S. Kirk Walsh for her excellent editing and careful mentoring. Kirk struggled to bring out the writer in me. I had a story to tell, and she helped me tremendously in the telling of it. Gina Williams, Joni Greeson, and Jeanine Brim were the first friends who encouraged me. Each read early drafts of my manuscript and provided valuable feedback. It was Joni who, after hearing one of my stories during a book club gathering, exclaimed, "You should write a memoir!"

I am indebted to Carol Ferguson, Nancy Shephard, Mandy Vickers, Beth West, Becky Wheeler, and David L. Berry for their early readings of the manuscript and helpful comments. And I am grateful for the superb editing skills of John McMurtrie. His fresh perspective and positive feedback gave me the confidence needed to finish my book.

I am most thankful to my patients and their families, who put their trust in me as their neonatologist over the course of three decades. Each parent I contacted about this book graciously and generously allowed me to share their child's story to illustrate my life and work in the NICU. In addition, each of my adult children granted permission to tell my version of their stories.

I am indebted to David Hancock of Morgan James Publishing; he believed in this book from the beginning. Thanks goes to Michael Ebeling for introducing me to David.

To my confidante and partner of thirty-seven years, Phillip, I am deeply grateful. He was and is my rock and was always there for our three children when I was not. I am eternally thankful to David, Anne, and Laura for sharing me with my patients and their families. All the time I spent in the hospital away from them was not without consequence. Each one of them provided me the love and freedom necessary to pursue my career. They are the ones who allowed me to live my physician life fully and practice as a neonatologist for more than thirty years. They are the ones who taught me to be a good enough mother.

DISCLAIMER

These stories of my patients and their parents have been altered to hide their identities. Wherever possible, the gender of the baby was changed. All the names used for patients and parents in this book are aliases, even though each parent gave me permission to reveal the identity and medical information about their child. The names of my colleagues and partners have also been changed to protect their identity.

"The first and truest thing is that all truth is a paradox. Life is filled with heartbreak and beauty, and many other things that are swirled together."

"Families are hard, hard, hard, no matter how cherished and astonishing they may also be.... Remember that in all cases, it's a miracle that any of us, specifically, were conceived and born. Earth is forgiveness school. It begins with forgiving yourself, and then you might as well start at the dinner table."

"We write to expose the unexposed. If there is one door in the castle you have been told not to go through, you must. Otherwise, you'll just be rearranging the furniture in rooms you've already been in. Most human beings are dedicated to keeping that one door shut. But the writer's job is to see what's behind it, to see the bleak unspeakable stuff, and to turn the unspeakable into words—not just into any words but if we can, into rhythm and blues. The truth of your experience can only come through in your own voice."

—Anne Lamott

INTRODUCTION

For thirty-five years, over countless days and nights, it was my privilege to take care of sick newborns and premature babies. I practiced neonatology, a subspecialty of pediatrics. My work was deeply inspiring and gratifying, but it could be dreadful, too, depending on the baby and the time of day or night. I have witnessed many extraordinary events in my career. Some patients were quite uneventful: babies came into the neonatal intensive care unit, got well, and went home quickly. This is not to say that their parents thought a short NICU stay was trivial. On the contrary. When your baby requires NICU care, it is generally terrifying for new parents.

Many of my favorite patients stayed longer, for weeks or months, and our time together was exceptional. They have names and stories that I will never forget. These babies and their parents often gave more to me than I was able to offer them. Life-and-death decisions are commonly made in the NICU and, as a result, one attempts to harden oneself against these. However, the burden of critical patient care is greater than you might imagine, and it can eclipse your personal priorities. That weight increases over time, and many years of practice may pass before the heaviness amasses. I found that my work always affected my attitude and frame of mind. Unfortunately, I became more cynical as my years of practice progressed.

I grew up in a small town in South Carolina but completed my medical training in two large cities in Texas. I met and married a native Texan and gave birth to our three children in Houston. My husband and I have been together, functioning as a team, for over thirty-six years. He is also a physician, was a well-respected pediatric nephrologist (a children's kidney disease specialist), and we were lucky to share several patients and practice in the same hospital on many occasions. He understood the demands of my work, and I understood his. Over the years, we enjoyed sharing stories about our patients and their parents. Each of us found solace in the other when our medical practice was stressful or demanding.

Without my husband I would not have been successful as a full-time working mother and physician. He unequivocally supported my practicing full-time. All working mothers struggle with child-care issues and work-life balance. I cannot imagine how single, working mothers survive. No matter what job a mother does, she inevitably, and at different times, must choose between her work and her family. Rarely can she pull off both at once. Practicing medicine puts a strain on motherhood, since one can argue that the patient always comes first. Doctors are taught this axiom as early as medical school. Understanding and voicing that commitment is one thing, but living it is something else entirely.

Both realms—practicing medicine and being a mother—evolved during the course of my career. I was a different doctor and mother at age thirty-three than I was at sixty. The road was rough at times, but I learned how to be a better doctor and mother as I grew older. My struggles taught me many lessons. For me, medicine and motherhood were woven together tightly to create the blended tapestry that illustrates my life's journey.

Chapter 1

PARENTAL WISHES

I t was August 1983. After finishing my three-year neonatal medicine fellowship in June, I found myself attending in the neonatal intensive care unit with one of my fellowship training professors. It was comforting that our NICU schedule paired together less experienced attendings, like me, with more seasoned neonatologists. Trevor was a brilliant, British-trained physician who performed sophisticated research on lung surfactant, and I admired both his research and teaching. He was tall and handsome, reticent and thoughtful. Having worked with him in the NICU many times before, I knew how he felt about critical care, living, and dying. He always chose living, sometimes opting to continue life support even though a case might appear to be hopeless.

After I completed my fellowship training, I felt differently. I had seen plenty of babies who were too critically ill, and too close to death, to survive. Their birth defects were inoperable, or their overwhelming infection spread to their brains, or their complications were too severe to predict any sort of functional life. I was well-trained, but still untested on my own in the NICU. Although everyone in the NICU knew that I was a competent fellow, I didn't feel competent yet as an attending neonatologist. I thought I still needed to prove myself to be excellent.

Trevor and I had daily rounds that August in the NICU, each with our own team of residents and fellows, and each of us attended to twelve to fifteen critically ill babies every day.

My team admitted a tiny baby a few days earlier. This little baby was amazingly stable, surviving on a ventilator, but his parents were not alright. An hour earlier, during NICU rounds, his nurse interrupted to report that they wanted to talk to me. After I finished my teaching rounds with the residents, having reviewed their care on all my patients, I approached the baby's bedside in the dimly lit, private NICU room. At once I noticed that his parents, a young couple standing arm in arm, seemed changed. The monitor softly beeped his regular heartbeats, and his blood pressure was normal. Two large catheters entered his umbilicus—his belly button—and one small IV was taped to the back of his tiny hand. A blood transfusion was in progress. A Saran Wrap blanket covered his entire body.

The previous two days had been a whirlwind for the couple: first, her emergency admission in active labor, followed quickly by their son's imminent preterm birth, his extreme size and medical condition, and his chances of survival going forward. This mother entered L&D—labor and delivery—with premature labor and rupture of membranes at twenty-three weeks gestation. Full term is forty weeks. She did not receive antenatal—before birth—steroids to mature his brain and lungs; there was not enough time. His birth occurred in the fall of 1983 before artificial surfactant was ubiquitous for treating respiratory distress in preterm infants. Their son weighed only 600 grams at birth—a little over one pound. I was aware that our NICU had very few survivors born that early and that small. However, the NICU team had attended mom's delivery two days before, and after a quick insertion of a breathing tube, whisked her baby away to the NICU for stabilization and continued care on a ventilator.

Theirs was a planned pregnancy; these parents had wanted a son very badly. They were both intelligent professionals, smart enough to handle the survival and outcome statistics that were explained to them in the L&D suite before his birth. In addition, this mother's uncle was a physician, and he confirmed their son's expected poor outcome and encouraged their reluctance to provide full support. This little boy was born below the current level of viability, which was then roughly twenty-five weeks gestation, yet here he was alive on a ventilator breathing for him, and no complications had yet arisen. That morning, his parents told me that they wanted to take their son off the ventilator. They seemed sad, but resolute.

Their request surprised me, but I was determined to help them work through their plight. Since I had recently finished my fellowship, I wanted to provide these parents with not only a compassionate ear, but also a correct and careful approach. I was hesitant to go about this the wrong way. So, we sat together by their son's bed and talked about their decision. I reviewed the current statistics describing his chances for survival and possible outcomes. They understood fully that most likely he would not survive; moreover, if he did, he would probably have an abnormal outcome. He had only a slim chance of normalcy. I believed that their choice was appropriate, but I knew that it was a rare set of parents who made this sort of decision early on in their child's care. Most lacked the courage to withdraw support.

After my discussion with them, I took Trevor aside to review the present dilemma with this baby. He listened quietly for a few minutes, then paused and warned me to "counsel the parents to proceed at all costs." This advice stunned me. I felt strongly that the parents' wishes should be considered, even honored at this extreme gestational age. At this time, I was not a parent myself, but I knew enough to seriously consider, and to respect, parents' wishes about their critically ill babies. The NICU ethicist had discussed this sort of clinical situation with us many times before. Perplexed about how to proceed—since I disagreed with Trevor—I called the chairperson of the hospital ethics committee to seek out her guidance. Dr. Desmond was a wonderful, white-haired neonatologist who ran the developmental follow-up clinic at our hospital. She was a well-respected, talented doctor. She always spoke with great passion about the outcomes of critically ill children and babies. I told her about my little patient, his parents, and my disagreement with Trevor. She encouraged me to present the case to the hospital ethics committee later that day. I agreed to do so with great apprehension.

At Texas Children's Hospital, the ethics committee consisted of an experienced general pediatrician, a pediatric subspecialist (usually a pediatric hematologist-oncologist), a pediatric intensive care physician, a medical ethicist, a developmental medicine specialist (the current chairperson), an experienced nurse, a parent whose child had received end-of-life care, and a hospital chaplain. Any physician or parent could convene the committee whenever conflicts arose in treatment decisions.

During lunch, I holed up in the neonatal conference room library and reviewed the outcomes of all babies born at twenty-three weeks gestation at our hospital in the prior two years—1981 to 1983. Only two of twelve such infants had survived, and those two had severe complications and were expected to grow up with major developmental disabilities. I eagerly went to find Trevor and recite these data to him. He listened carefully, but was unmoved, and mumbled something about "expecting outcomes to improve each year." Then he gave me a look that gave me the distinct feeling that he was disappointed in me for even considering the parents' wishes. Disappointing your attending, especially one who was your teacher, is uncomfortable, and I had not been in this position before. After looking at two years' worth of our hospital data, I personally agreed with the parents' plan to withdraw support and allow their son to die of his extreme prematurity.

Later that afternoon, I nervously presented his case to the hospital ethics committee. Everyone convened around the oval wood table in a large conference room within Dr. Desmond's office, and the discussions I heard were both academic and realistic. I watched and listened, unsure of the outcome, and the committee voted unanimously to support the parents' plan to remove their son from his ventilator. At that moment I was relieved and felt empowered and justified in allowing them to make this decision.

Later that evening, his nurse helped me turn off and disconnect the infusions. We carefully loosened the tape on his nose and upper lip, and I removed the breathing tube from this precious little boy—a fetus, really. I wrapped him in a soft, blue blanket, and handed him to his mother and father. His mom sat comfortably in a nearby rocking chair, surrounded by stuffed pillows, her feet propped on a low stool. Dad sat very close by. This was the first time she held him since birth. Mom lifted him up, wrapped in his blanket, for a kiss. Both mom and dad cried and spoke gently to him. I wish that I could remember his name. It was obvious that they loved and wanted him very much.

There were no other family members available, so I asked if I could sit with them, and was honored when they agreed. He seemed comfortable in their arms while his mother stroked his little hands and face. That evening I sat there with that young couple, watching them hold their son—loving him and saying goodbye—for three hours. It was heartbreaking. I kept thinking—what if this were my husband and me? Would we be doing the same thing? Gradually, his weak breathing stopped, then his heart rate slowed, and finally his heart stopped beating, and he died. I believe this was the most difficult and excruciating decision that couple ever made. In my mind, their decision was correct for them, but I felt drained.

After pronouncing the baby dead and signing all the necessary forms, I left the hospital and drove home to my husband, Phillip. He had dinner waiting for me, and a glass of wine. I cried as I recounted the story of my day—Trevor's comments, my feelings of disappointment, my nervousness going before the ethics committee, my fears about doing the wrong thing, how kind Dr. Desmond had been, all of it. He listened patiently and reassured me that those parents and I had done the right thing in deciding to let that baby go. He told me that I was brave to want to help them. I cried some more as the reality of attending such critically ill cases settled over me. Would I be up to the demands of a life in the NICU, the endless hours, the worried parents, the constant alarms, and the ethical dilemmas? Since Phillip was three years ahead of me in training and experience (he was a pediatric nephrologist at the same hospital), that evening I felt soothed by his assurances.

About a year later, I was the young mother in premature labor at twenty-five weeks gestation, in our own L&D unit. My son, David, might be born extremely premature. I was terrified. How could this have happened to me? Within the first year of my marriage, I unexpectedly conceived. We both wanted a baby, but since I was thirty-four at the time, I thought it would take longer. However, any joy that I felt about being pregnant was overwhelmed by my endless and terrible nausea and vomiting. I threw up every morning before work, usually able to keep down only Coca-Cola and peanut butter spread on saltine crackers. I threw up during daily rounds in the NICU because the phototherapy lights that we shined on the babies to treat their jaundice made me feel queasy. If my team and

I walked past a bank of those special blue fluorescent lights, I immediately felt sick and ran to a nearby trash can to vomit. My residents were often amused by this behavior, but I was determined to continue working through my rocky first trimester.

My pregnancy proceeded along with unrelenting nausea and vomiting for twelve long weeks while I worked in the NICU full time. I survived on only crackers, peanut butter, and Coke. We were both excited when the ultrasound at eighteen weeks gestation revealed that we were having a boy. However, I found myself frightened during the amniocentesis procedure. During amniocentesis, a sample of amniotic fluid is obtained by ultrasound guidance and sent for genetic testing. Having observed amnioclenteses performed many times, I felt confident that mine would be routine. During the procedure, though, I was truly anxious watching that large needle being stuck into me, and I worried that it might stick the baby.

After my nausea resolved and the genetics test came back normal, we adjusted to the idea of having a son. Like most other pregnant women, I began to enjoy being pregnant and envisioned having a perfectly normal, healthy full-term baby. I remember being worried about catching some terrible germ from one of my NICU patients but realized that I was probably making up things to worry about. My husband kept telling me I was overthinking things. Then at twenty-four weeks I noticed twinges of pain low down in my uterus, off and on in the afternoons. The pains were worse after a long or difficult day in the NICU, especially after standing to perform procedures. If I went home and put my feet up, the pains would usually subside. All my prenatal check-ups had been normal, and then my premature labor commenced in earnest at twenty-five weeks gestation.

After rounding in the NICU one morning, I was feeling particularly tired, and my pelvic pains were really hurting. I ran into my own obstetrician, a good friend and colleague. He took me by the hand to L&D to examine me. I did not expect what happened next. After finding that my cervix was dilated and I was in active preterm labor, he admitted me to the hospital. I was not prepared for that. No mother is ever prepared for the trauma of a pregnancy complication. All I could think about was having a tiny premature baby boy who would require

NICU care for months on end. Of course, I imagined the worst-case scenario. I fully understood the long haul of intensive care that a tiny premature infant must endure for survival, and I dreaded the idea of watching my son go through this. Also, I feared the possibility of raising a disabled child. An artificial surfactant trial was being conducted in our NICU at that time, one of Trevor's studies. If enrolled in this trial, our son would have a fifty-fifty chance of receiving the life-saving surfactant treatment. That was a good thing.

I called my husband, who came directly to find me in L&D. My labor room was freezing, and he found me shivering with cold and fear. He asked the nurses to get me a blanket and a sedative. Then he went over to the NICU to see which neonatologist was on call, who would be working with us if our son delivered prematurely during the night. It was Trevor, the same partner who had disagreed with my decision to support those parents in their choice to let their son go at twenty-three weeks gestation. Oh, God, I thought. Trevor and Phillip talked. Unbelievably, he told Phillip that he would do everything possible for David if he was born that evening, even if we disagreed with his approach. He also said that he would only give the life-saving surfactant if the randomization sequence of his study indicated that selection, and that under no circumstances would he deviate from the study design. That I understood, but his not respecting our wishes, I did not. Now I was more bewildered than ever.

Phillip sought out other professional opinions while I fretted in my room. In the dark and chilly labor suite, I lay crying, imagining the worst as I listened to David's soft heartbeat on the uterine monitor. Another one of my older partners, a friend of Phillip's from residency, popped in to visit and caught me crying. He smiled and asked, "Susan, what are you so upset about?" I didn't answer at first and felt somewhat baffled that he even asked. Did I need to justify my fears? Wasn't I allowed some normal maternal tears? Of course, he tried to reassure me that everything would be alright, but I remained terribly frightened, and he stepped out to go find my husband.

In our personal encounter with possible preterm delivery, we got lucky, and all turned out well. My aggressive perinatologist—a high-risk obstetrician—and friend expertly directed my care. Two powerful medications effectively stopped my premature labor, and I received antenatal steroids to mature my son's lungs and brain. My obstetrician also prescribed valium for me, intermittently, since I felt trapped in a net of excessive worry. Of course, then I worried about possible effects of valium on my unborn son.

After two days, once my preterm labor was deemed under control, they moved me to a room on the obstetrical floor. I remember disliking the residents' morning rounds, since someone always wanted to feel my pregnant uterus. My private room was sunny and comfortable, but too close to the NICU. As a result, I received too many visitors during the day, and it became impossible to rest. So, the nurses taped signs on the door to keep visitors out. After a hospital stay of several weeks, I was permitted to go home. I discovered later that while I was in the hospital, all my peers, the other neonatologists and nurse practitioners, had a lottery running about my delivery date. They wagered on the date that I would deliver emergently during the night, and the loser would have to be my baby's doctor.

At home I was able to rest, read, and listen to soothing New Age music. I imagined myself to be a large vessel, a pregnant uterus, whose purpose was one thing—to make this baby. I had never imagined myself to be something so simple and yet so complex. Phillip cooked and brought meals to our upstairs bedroom. His mother came to help us out since I was instructed to stay in bed except for bathroom breaks. Surprisingly, it was not easy to lie around and do nothing all day. It was certainly not easy to be pleasant with my mother-in-law hovering over me, but I put great effort into being nice to her. Previously, she acted as if she didn't like me that much. Once when my husband, then my fiancé, told her that I was a doctor, she remarked, "What's wrong with her? Why isn't she a nurse?" It's very revealing that my sweet mother-in-law did not really begin to like me until I became a mother myself. She then became one of my biggest fans.

I remained on bed rest at home for several weeks. Phillip and his mother took very good care of me. David was delivered at thirty-six weeks gestation, late one Friday night, only a month before my due date. Although we stayed in the hospital for a week, he never needed artificial surfactant or NICU care, and he had a perfectly normal outcome. The experience of being a patient myself, particularly a pregnant-mother-patient, taught me a tremendous lesson. The degree of helplessness that you feel in that situation is difficult to describe. Your powerlessness seems inexorable if you are a trained and competent person used to getting things done or accustomed to solving problems.

I had witnessed many irresponsible, unwed, teen mothers with little to no prenatal care give birth to perfectly healthy full-term babies, without even trying. Here I was an educated neonatologist, who had done everything right, and yet I could not carry a baby correctly to term. My feelings of inadequacy and vulnerability during that time were boundless. I felt like a big fat failure throughout most of my first pregnancy, and I was determined to make up for that by being a perfect mother.

Later, throughout my years of practice in neonatology, as I met and counseled other mothers anticipating a preterm delivery, it was easy to empathize with them. I understood the feelings of fear and helplessness they endured through that most traumatic time. Over the years, I gladly shared my own story with mothers in preterm labor, or those with premature rupture of membranes, as they lay in hospital beds, receiving various kinds of treatment, awaiting the birth of their own baby. When I recounted my story to them, many of them felt understood and grateful. Sometimes even the smallest sharing of feelings provided them with some comfort.

Chapter 2

LIFE IN THE NICU

My eight-week maternity leave was practically blissful. David was a good baby and caring for him was easy. My first experience with breastfeeding went well from the beginning, mainly because I was lucky. I was accustomed to being awake and up at night (from all the previous NICU night calls during residency and fellowship), and I learned to take naps during the day, so I did not suffer much from sleep deprivation during my fourth trimester. I was extremely happy that he was alive, healthy, and closer to full-term than we ever expected, so much so that pure contentment carried me through those first two months.

However, once my baby was two months old, I returned to work and the NICU cases came screaming back. I immediately took over the care of one critically ill baby with persistent pulmonary hypertension of the newborn, known as PPHN. He was the two-day-old son of a young elementary school teacher, born post-dates at forty-one weeks gestation, very scrawny and thin, and he developed severe respiratory distress. He had been stressed in utero (a result of low oxygen levels from poor placental function) and, as a result, had inhaled meconium (the baby's first dark green stool) into his lungs. The low oxygen levels the baby endured in utero caused increased pulmonary (lung) artery pressures. This caused his blood to shunt the wrong way at two points within his heart.

On my first day back to work, the inhaled meconium obstructed his airways, and he developed an acute pneumothorax (literally, air in the chest). When air leaked from his injured lung into the chest cavity, it caused collapse of the adjacent lung, and his blood pressure, oxygen level, and heart rate plummeted. This was an emergency. I quickly inserted a chest tube in between the baby's ribs to provide continuous drainage of the air leak. There was no time to ask permission. Thankfully, the procedure was straightforward and successful. With the chest tube functioning, he settled down onto reasonable respiratory support and his vital signs stabilized. Then I went to talk with his mother and father about the chest tube and vividly remember being aware of my painful, throbbing, engorged breasts. I forgot to take a break to pump my milk during all the morning's tension. Their son was so ill throughout my first day back that I settled in at his bedside for several hours and did not leave to eat lunch or pump my breast milk. I resumed my personal routine in the NICU of hovering at a critically ill baby's bedside—watching, thinking, teaching—and for good reason.

PPHN babies normally require constant attention. In the past they were paralyzed (given a drug to make them stop moving and breathing) and supported on aggressive ventilator settings. They needed sedation, of course, because they were awake and could feel things; they were just not moving or breathing. We did all the breathing for them. The drugs we used back then to lower pulmonary artery pressures also lowered systemic, or whole body, blood pressure. As a result, these babies needed lots of blood transfusions and other fluids and medicines to support their blood pressure and kidney function. These were some of our sickest newborns. It was tough to talk with parents about blood transfusions back in the 1980s, after HIV had emerged. Profound patience and reassurance were required to convince them of the blood's safety. (PPHN babies are not as challenging to care for today, since we have inhaled nitric oxide, a wonder drug discovered in the early 1990s. Nitric oxide is a gas that effectively lowers pulmonary artery pressures, working directly within the lung, once it is pumped into the ventilator.)

During that busy week back in the NICU, I continued to struggle with engorgement. My breasts hurt constantly and when I heard a baby cry—any baby—my milk let down, giving me a warm, tingly feeling, soaking my breast pads, and staining my dress or scrubs. Clearly, I was lousy with this pumping-at-work routine. The few times when I did manage to escape to my office, shut the door, and begin pumping, I used a small hand-held, battery-operated pump. There were few good pumps available back then, except for the hospital-grade electric breast pumps. I don't know why I didn't take advantage of the hospital's electric pumps. Maybe they were all in use by the NICU moms. I probably considered myself too busy with my sick babies. Not taking advantage of those breast pumps, however, turned out to be a big mistake.

The teacher's baby with PPHN recovered slowly over that first week. Other sick babies continued to be admitted, and there was plenty of work to do—checking labs and X-rays, writing orders, adjusting ventilator settings, performing procedures, supervising residents, attending high-risk deliveries, responding to alarms and parents' requests for information. I liked being busy again. I had always enjoyed the activity and thrum of the NICU, and this time was no different. It was the necessary periodic pumping of breast milk that was so challenging. Every time my breasts throbbed, or let down milk, I thought of my baby and felt guilty. Fortunately, I was able to nurse him in the evening after I returned home from work, again during the night, and before leaving for work the next day. But that didn't suffice.

On the Friday of my first week back in the NICU, I pulled into the parking lot at 7:30 a.m., feeling satisfied with how the week had gone. Julie, one of the NNPs—a neonatal nurse practitioner—paged me to relay a message: "One of your preemies just perf'ed." This is shorthand for perforated, meaning that a hole had ruptured in her intestine, allowing stool contents to spill into her abdominal cavity. "Oh shoot," I said, pounding on the steering wheel. I parked and rushed through the ER, hurried up to the NICU, and swiped my ID badge across the electronic scanner. There was a loud clunk as the huge NICU doors opened, one swinging in, the other swinging out. I raced into the unit without scrubbing in to find Art, my partner who worked the previous night. He was at her bedside in one of the back bays, writing orders for dopamine, a medication to support blood pressure. Julie was already scrubbed and gowned for a sterile procedure, an attempt to insert a central line into a vein in her right arm. Knowing that I was on my way, the nurses gathered up the necessary supplies for insertion of an arterial catheter into her left wrist, one of my favorite procedures.

Little Emily looked horrible. Her abdomen was dusky gray, bloated, and tightly swollen like a bulging drum. She was already intubated and on a ventilator for life support. Her heart rate was too high and her blood pressure too low. A small dose of morphine had not changed her heart rate, but she did not appear to be in pain. She laid quietly on her back, spread-eagle, allowing us to work on her. The large, chunky portable X-ray machine was still parked near her bed, reminding me of a front-loader tractor ready for road work.

I asked if mom had been called. When Art said, "No, not yet," I paused to quickly phone her. The baby's mother awoke slowly as I introduced myself and told her there was some bad news. Then I described what happened to her daughter and beckoned her to come into the hospital to speak with the pediatric surgeon before Emily's emergency abdominal surgery later that morning. She reminded me that her husband was out of town on a business trip. I reassured her that we would go over everything again and promised that we would call her husband once she arrived. Then I turned to wash my hands and within fifteen minutes, I had threaded the thin arterial catheter into her tiny wrist artery and secured it in place. The nurses then attached the proper fluids and blood pressure monitor.

Once Art completed his checkout with the other neonatologist present that day, he and I discussed what had happened to Emily, and reviewed any overnight changes with my other patients. Art was headed home, but I would remain in the NICU for the next twenty-four hours. This was my first scheduled twenty-four-hour shift and Friday night call since returning to work. After my long, peaceful stint at home with my baby, this felt overwhelming.

At this time, the NICU was filled with many other babies. There were two sick, full-term babies with group B Streptococcal sepsis (bloodstream infection) and pneumonia, some larger premature infants convalescing (we called them "feeder-growers"), and various other babies ill from congenital birth defects. Ventilators were pumping breaths into and out of babies with respiratory distress.

High-frequency oscillators were jiggling the chests of the two sickest babies, one a "micropreemie" and the other a gigantic eleven-pound infant of a diabetic mother. Our NICU cared for a mix of the smallest preemies alongside bigger term babies with congenital heart defects and various lung diseases. Usually, it was a tolerable balance of patients and a mix of conditions that offered something interesting for everyone on staff.

Emily's father arrived to join his wife just as the pediatric surgeon completed the procedure and saved her life that Friday. Because Emily had an isolated intestinal perforation—not necrotizing enterocolitis, a severe bowel inflammatory condition)—she would continue to recover with antibiotics and rest. After the surgery, her parents seemed reassured and grateful. Mom's relief was evident through her tears. These were typical NICU parents—young, married, and never expecting a premature baby. They had endured her early respiratory distress and need for ventilator support at birth, all the lines and tubes, the possible infections, and the initiation of feedings. Emily conquered each challenge and was off the ventilator and recovering nicely until now. As a result, some days her parents were happy and optimistic, and other days they were distressed, like today.

Dad looked despondent as he told me, "She was fine yesterday. That's why I left on my trip." He probably felt guilty because she suddenly deteriorated during his absence. This pattern of stabilization, improvement, then—wham, a complication—was a phenomenon that a lot of NICU parents experienced. They described this roller-coaster of emotions as the most stressful time of their lives as new parents. Parents were forever present, visiting, waiting, and hoping. Some rocked quietly next to their baby's bed, others stood and hovered close by, asking questions and looking scared. Worried grandparents were part of the mix as well, and the nurses would come and fetch us to give all of them updates throughout the day.

Every NICU has a sound and a feel to it. Sometimes noise bounced off the ceiling or floor. When the nurses prepared for a surgical case within the unit, like Emily's, things tended to get loud. At other times, the NICU was calm, dimly lit, and quiet. Large windows lined the unit on either side, which gave the NICU less of a boxed-in feeling. The walls were painted lavender or light blue, supposedly relaxing colors. Throughout the mornings, the lumbering X-ray machine was pushed from bed to bed, nurses prepared fluids and helped with procedures, and doctors wrote orders and called consultants.

The NICU featured large rooms or bays lined with large warming beds or incubators placed along the walls; sometimes two or four beds were grouped together. Equipment crowded both sides of each bed, usually two or three IV pumps fastened to stainless steel poles, and a ventilator on a rolling stand surrounded most warmers holding the sickest babies. Each baby was nestled in and cared for in the middle of the warming bed, the smallest ones under a blanket of Saran Wrap. Larger, more stable babies were swaddled inside see-through plastic incubators. Sometimes a cloth blanket was draped over the incubator to lessen light exposure.

The NICU held monitors galore, sounding heartbeats and alarms. Rocking chairs, bins for trash and soiled linens were scattered about, and boxes of exam gloves were placed throughout the unit. Two computer stations were positioned within each bay, and several portable computer carts rolled about. The X-ray machine usually lived in the hall just outside the unit near the blood gas lab. Nowadays, some NICUs provide single-use rooms, so that parents can sleep over and have some privacy with their sick newborn. (I cannot imagine how the parents get any rest staying there overnight.)

We neonatologists divided the patients among us and rotated taking admissions throughout each day. A typical NICU shift consisted of attending to twelve to fifteen sick babies and rounding with pediatric residents or an NNP. There were occasional consultations in the newborn nursery that called us away. Each morning I examined babies, wrote orders for medications and intravenous nutrition, calculated hyperalimentation fluids, and prescribed feedings. Morning rounds with residents or NNP's were demanding and time-consuming. Many patient explanations were required. We ordered diagnostic tests, most of which were performed at the bedside, like chest and abdominal X-rays and ultrasounds. Blood gases (actual blood levels of pH, oxygen, and carbon dioxide) were checked and ventilator settings adjusted. We inserted various kinds of catheters and tubes into the sickest babies, depending on clinical necessity. Each of these procedures were taught to residents or NNPs before they could perform them alone without direct supervision.

Some of the attending neonatologists I worked with were notorious. At Texas Children's Hospital there was one brilliant neonatologist and professor, Dr. John Adamson, who was a whiz at mechanical ventilation. He used the ventilator and various medications to resurrect the most hopelessly ill babies back to stability and recovery. But he was also a firecracker. Stupidity set him off quicker than anything else. He was a slim man with black hair and a trimmed, salt-and-pepper beard. His long shirtsleeves were always rolled up to just above his elbows. Dr. Adamson would stand at the bedside with his arms folded tightly across his chest and repeatedly rock back and forth on his feet, bouncing from his toes to his heels. That posture and his presence made him infamous at the hospital. You could easily visualize his red-faced fury about to erupt. On morning rounds, after hearing a resident's disorganized presentation, he was fond of saying things like, "Even the janitor could have done a better job." He commonly wore street clothes in the NICU and placed a cloth cover gown over them. One day, when his short fuse had been lit by some poor resident, he reached for a pen in his shirt pocket but could not retrieve it since the cover gown was in the way. He grabbed some scissors from a bedside table, cut a hole in the gown right over his breast pocket, took out his pen, and wrote an order.

In the hospital's NICU, I worked Monday through Friday from 8 a.m. to 6 p.m., then rounded for several hours on Saturday and Sunday. The neo fellows covered Monday through Thursday nights and weekend call nights. The attendings shared Friday night calls. After twelve straight days of work in the NICU, we earned our weekend off, and then the pattern repeated itself. The daytime hours spent in the hospital added up to fifty to seventy per week, depending on vacations and holidays. It was a demanding schedule, although not as bad as some we survived during fellowship. We also rotated our attendance of high-risk deliveries, usually going to L&D with the NNP. They liked to attend deliveries more than the residents so that they could insert catheters and breathing tubes into sick babies.

Attending a delivery meant that two or three of us don cap, mask, gown, and sterile gloves, and, using a sterile towel, we would "catch" the baby handed to one of us by the delivering obstetrician. The baby was then taken to a nearby warmer for assessment and necessary support. Whenever pediatric residents were our helpers, they required lots of supervision and teaching. With an eager resident, this process was usually pleasant, but some were timid, and their performance of procedures demanded considerable coaxing and extra time. Admissions of sick babies born in L&D typically occurred intermittently throughout the day. Sometimes stable babies took a turn for the worse and became critically ill babies, like little Emily, who unexpectedly perforated her bowel.

It was common to attend the delivery of a high-risk mother with chorioamnionitis (intrauterine infection) and premature labor, or suffering from severe preeclampsia (pregnancy induced hypertension), shepherd her extremely preterm baby into the NICU, insert lines and tubes, and provide fluids and medications—only to witness her baby deteriorate from a massive intraventricular hemorrhage (bleeding into the brain) or pulmonary hemorrhage (bleeding into the lungs) around twenty-four to forty-eight hours of age. Most of those tiny babies died shortly thereafter.

Overnight on call in the NICU, we wore short-sleeved, soft, blue cotton hospital scrubs. These were comfortable and easy to clean. During the day I wore street clothes with a thin, cotton cover gown placed over them. This outfit was too hot, but adequately protected my clothes from pee and poop. Our scrubs and white coats were embroidered with our name and the name of our practice group. I wore a small, black, neonatal stethoscope hanging around my neck all the time. It came in handy for emergency deliveries and quick consults in the newborn nursery. My stethoscope had to be cleaned with alcohol between each use, however. To decrease chances for contamination, each baby in the NICU had their own red stethoscope hanging on their bed.

Most often we examined and cared for newly admitted babies on a radiant warming bed that had two long banks of radiant heat sources positioned along either side, three feet above the bed. The bed had a thermostat mechanism that was attached by wire to a skin probe positioned on the baby's abdomen. The bed's output kept the baby exactly at 36.4 degrees Centigrade, by switching the overhead heaters on or off, as needed. This work environment tended to dry out your eyes or burn the top of your head if you were not careful. During long procedures, my contact lenses felt like potato chips, and I found myself drenched in sweat. From the start, I disliked wearing makeup in the NICU.

Makeup tended to smear, and mascara irritated my already dry contacts. When running to an emergency delivery, the process of putting on a surgical gown, throwing on a hair bonnet, stuffing your hair up into it, adjusting the mask over your nose and mouth, and tying the strings always made a mess of hair and makeup, so I gave it up.

The NICU at Texas Children's Hospital was an isolated unit within the hospital and often felt like its own little world. Escapes to the bathroom, lounge, or cafeteria were rare. Teaching pediatric residents and NNPs required patience, not a characteristic that came naturally to me (although I never cut holes in a cover gown). I liked things done fast and done effectively. In the NICU, interruptions were interminable, and the multitasking was endless. We consulted with other subspecialists, pediatric surgeons, pediatric urologists, pediatric cardiologists, nephrologists, neurologists, hematologists, pulmonologists, geneticists, and infectious diseases specialists. I enjoyed chatting with consultants when they entered the unit and felt a sense of comradery concerning difficult patients. We talked to parents often, usually at the bedside, but also in a mother's room when she was ill herself. Every procedure required a consent form filled out, signed, and witnessed, after a discussion of risks and benefits with at least one parent. The NICU nurses were bulldogs—in a good way—at enforcing that consent had been properly obtained and documented.

I had been back at work for several weeks, and my NICU work life seemed routine, when suddenly I was confronted with caring for a set of conjoined twins transferred in from Mexico. It was 1985 and I had no understanding of that condition, and at that time I was working with Dr. Adamson, who was one of my teachers and a harsh critic during my fellowship. As these baby girls rolled into the NICU, I looked at him sheepishly as if to say, "Help." He looked at me, grinned, and replied, "I already passed this test. It's your turn." So, I grabbed an NNP for help and we proceeded to assess the twins.

The baby girls laid on their sides together in one bed, facing each other, fused throughout their entire abdomen. It was astonishing to see them lying there: two heads pointed upward and each baby with her arms wrapped around her sister. Four legs and feet pointed downward. Each girl was connected to her own set of lines and tubes, and all of those made for quite a tangle. One twin had severe congenital heart disease, was unstable, and would likely die soon. Her blood pressure was low, and her single kidney was failing. The other baby had a normal heart, most of the liver that her sister shared, and one kidney that seemed structurally sound.

The admission of one newly transferred-in unstable baby, much less two, took hours of constant bedside attention and care, lingering over the warming bed, checking lab values and chest X-rays, adjusting the ventilator or medication drips. Your other patients had to wait, for a while, or be seen by another physician, resident, or NNP. I was terrified of these twin girls. Over the next day, the pediatric cardiologists and pediatric surgeons worked together to evaluate each girl's organs—shared and otherwise—and to propose a plan for the family. I appreciated listening in and hearing the explanations of the older, more experienced subspecialists. The parents spoke only Spanish, so translators were required for every encounter. The surgical teams recommended separation of both girls. They all agreed and described to the parents that separation would save the one with the least malformations, but that the one with inoperable heart defect would die.

However, this young Latina, Catholic mother wanted nothing of their plan. In the meantime, the more severely affected baby continued to deteriorate and made her still-connected sister even sicker. For two days, their mother could not abide the idea of separating her twins and "killing" the sicker baby. She wept openly as she lingered at their bedside. All throughout this ordeal I was overwhelmed and felt unprepared to contribute to this situation or support her. I felt I had little to offer her except a knowing, sad look. However, the NICU ethicist guided me and the NNP through the process, while the chaplain somehow convinced mom that it was okay to let one baby go, in order to save the other. Otherwise they both would die.

On day three, the two girls were separated during a long and complicated surgery. The weaker twin died in the operating room soon thereafter, but the stronger twin returned to the NICU, stabilized, and began to recover. Only then was I able to relax and appreciate being part of a team of pediatric surgeons, pediatric cardiologists, social worker, chaplain, and neonatal ethicist who had enough patience to deal with these parents. In caring for these conjoined twins, my team saved me, too. My role as the neonatologist had been easy, controlling the ventilator settings, adjusting fluids, and medications. It was the chaplain who provided the greatest impact in this case. Over the following two weeks, I was pleased to witness the surviving twin girl grow stronger, and her mother grow more accepting of her. Her mother began to visit, smile, and hold her more often, and she surprised us one Sunday by having her christened right there in the NICU. This was a good sign that she accepted the blessing of her daughter's life. (In contrast, most christenings in the NICU occurred before the imminent death of a baby.) And before long, that little girl was stable enough to fly back home to Mexico City with her parents.

Many other babies born with a major birth defect in other hospitals around Houston were transferred into our NICU for evaluation and care. I admitted and cared for many babies with spina bifida, a midline malformation of the neural tube. Some of these babies had quite severe, high defects that involved the spinal cord and major spinal nerves. All their organs below the level of the defect were affected, so proper bowel and kidney function rarely occurred. Even after surgical repair, some never recovered any movement of their legs. Many were plagued with hydrocephalus (spinal fluid backed up within the brain) requiring surgical shunts, and often these shunts became infected.

A different congenital malformation, called gastroschisis, was equally challenging and afflicted babies in different ways. Gastroschisis is an abdominal wall defect in which the intestines develop outside of the fetal body and are injured in utero while floating freely in the alkaline amniotic fluid. After birth, the intestines are returned to the abdomen and the abdominal wall defect is surgically repaired. However, the injured intestines take weeks to recover proper function. Afflicted babies required continuous IV hyperalimentation (nutrition) until their bowel function returned to normal and they could be fed. Once feedings were begun, and tolerated, they were advanced ever so slowly. The entire process often took six to eight weeks.

Another abdominal wall malformation that we saw often, called omphalocele, was generally less severe because those babies were born with a protective membrane covering their protruding intestines. Early in my career I assisted in the care of a full-term baby with a giant omphalocele the size of a cantaloupe.

Her pediatric surgeon instructed our nurses to paint her covering membrane with mercurochrome to thicken it and to provide antisepsis. Because her membrane covering was thin, the baby unexpectedly absorbed mercury from that product. She developed symptoms of mercury poisoning and turned a bright orangey-pink color all over, just like a salmon. Unfortunately, that little girl did not survive her inadvertent mercury exposure. It was unforgettable to witness such a profound detrimental drug effect.

Maternal heroin addiction was rampant in the 1980s. As a result, I took care of numerous babies with neonatal abstinence syndrome, a condition in which the newborn withdraws from intrauterine exposure to maternal drugs. Those babies coughed, sneezed, and trembled. Some rubbed their knees raw in their cribs and screamed shrill cries. Many had fever, diarrhea, or spit up, and the worst cases had seizures. These withdrawing babies were extremely sensitive to light and sound, so we kept them together in dimly lit, quiet isolation rooms. They ate badly and gained weight poorly. Even the mothers who attempted to get help and were on a methadone replacement program had babies who withdrew brutally from that drug. Usually, it took six to eight weeks for them to wean off their mother's narcotics, stop shaking and trembling, eat well enough to gain weight, and go home.

Back then we provided tincture of opium drops by mouth as the baby's replacement drug. Today we use oral morphine and calculate tiny doses meticulously, weaning down by ten to fifteen percent every other day. The baby's weaning (abstinence or withdrawal) process usually takes weeks. I remember feeling judgmental toward those drug-addicted mothers and caring for their babies tested my compassion. Decades ago, drug addiction was thought of as a personal or moral failing, and sometimes I caught myself looking condescendingly at those mothers. Today we know better and recognize addiction to narcotics, such as oxycodone or heroin, as a severe disease that hijacks the mother's brain.

The variety of newborn conditions that I encountered and cared for during the early years of my career was astounding, and always challenging, but also gratifying. It was a privilege to attend to sick babies in a NICU at a reputable children's hospital, one affiliated with a renowned medical school that drew patients from the surrounding metropolitan area. I felt reassured to be working with other faculty attendings who possessed great knowledge and experience, even if they did, on occasion, have a temper. Even though I was a neonatology attending, I was still learning, gaining skills, and confidence. In retrospect, it took almost two years after completing my fellowship to feel truly confident in my skills as a clinician.

My first few months as a physician mother in the NICU were filled with both adventure and heartache. I loved taking care of sick newborns. It was both fascinating and thrilling. Watching little babies respond to treatments was gratifying. Punctuated within those routine NICU cases, unfortunately, were those unfortunate babies who died from severe respiratory distress or succumbed to unexpected complications, like a massive hemorrhage into the brain. Sitting quietly with parents during and after the death of their baby was heartbreaking—every time—whether the baby had died from mercury poisoning, group B strep sepsis, or severe respiratory distress. Sometimes after my workday ended, I would drive home to my young son, hold him, and cry with fatigue and discouragement. In the NICU, each of us knew that we would be confronted with babies who could not be saved. Thankfully, there were vastly more infants who responded well to treatment, recovered, and thrived. Those varying sorts of NICU clinical situations, the intensive care paradox in which some patients lived, and some died, profoundly shaped my nascent character as a neonatologist caring for critically ill neonates.

Chapter 3

MATERNAL AWAKENING

Becoming a mother is nothing like becoming a doctor. Unlike medical school and residency, there is no protracted period of preparation, no mothers' school, or mothering residency program. You have a baby and boom—you're a mother. If you're lucky, you may have time to read about or research pregnancy, childbirth, and early childhood development. No one was around to teach me about breastfeeding, my mother offered little helpful advice, and this was before the Internet. Back then, it was simple to understand why young mothers, including me, knew so little about breastfeeding. The generation before us had not breastfed, as a rule, so they were unable to inform us of the correct ways to go about it and could not support us through our breastfeeding problems. They fed formula to their infants, so when anything went wrong, the inevitable answer was "Why don't you just use formula?"

I felt lucky that David was such an easy baby. One of my best friends, a neonatologist at Baylor College of Medicine, was miserable caring for her colicky first-born son, and I felt so sorry for her. He cried for several hours every afternoon. By contrast, my son took long naps and never cried much, most likely because I never put him down. I read that babies who were held and carried around often were calmer and better attached to their mothers. I had no special knowledge or training in infant attachment, however in all that free time available to me during my threatening premature labor, I read many books about infant attachment and child development—those by Erickson, Piaget, Montessori, Brazelton and others.

Cuddling with my newborn son was a great joy. His skin was velvety soft and covered with fine, downy lanugo, or newborn hair. The dark, silky hair on his head stuck out wildly in every direction. He had the cutest little dimple, a divot really, on the outside of his right ear lobule, and a matching stork bite on the right side of his neck behind that ear. (Of course, all new mothers examine every aspect of their newborn's body.) I loved to rock my son to sleep, then place him all curled up on his tummy in his crib in a room adjacent to our bedroom. Remote control sound monitors didn't exist back then, but I didn't need one— he was close enough that I could hear his fingernails scratching on the crib sheet at night. It was a good thing that I was a light sleeper then. I awoke easily and went to him just as he started making those soft sounds— "ehh, ehh, ehh"— before he started crying.

We know now that crying is a late sign of hunger, and that it is more difficult to calm and feed a crying baby compared to one who is just beginning to awaken. I benefited from having read about hunger cues. Many new moms are unaware that a baby is hungry when he licks his lips, sticks out his tongue, puts his fist into his mouth, or jerks his head around to the side after his cheek is stroked. Feeding a baby then is certainly easier than after he begins crying. In addition, prone positioning—having a baby sleep on his tummy—is frowned upon today and considered unsafe, but back then we didn't know any better. I swaddled him in a blanket effectively, having been taught that skill by the hospital nursery nurses years before.

Contrary to current recommendations, I allowed my son to nurse in bed with me. Initially, while still learning how to breastfeed, I would get up with him, change his diaper, and nurse him every three hours throughout the night while seated in a stuffed recliner rocker. Once I learned how to effectively nurse side-lying, I would return to bed and nurse him there as we both fell back asleep. That was so comfortable—for me and him—but side-lying breastfeeding is a difficult, learned skill. Although lots of moms today nurse in bed and co-sleep with their babies, it is currently frowned upon and thought to be a form of unsafe sleep.

I genuinely enjoyed my time at home with my son after his birth and remember being tired but rarely exhausted. After four years of taking NICU night call, I was used to being up at night. I learned to take power naps during my residency and fellowship training. The adage "sleep when the baby sleeps" is true, and I became serious about sleep during my maternity leave, to the point of sometimes even denying visitors. I would also let the phone ring when I was napping. Most folks called back again in the evening when my husband was home. Some mothers have tremendous problems with the many weeks of sleep deprivation that come with caring for a newborn.

I felt a huge sense of relief to have a healthy baby after my traumatic and abnormal pregnancy. Thankfully, I was not afraid of my baby, and instantly fell in love with him. Despite being born one month early, he breastfed easily, and acted like one of those "good" sleepy babies who never seemed to cry and stayed on the breast for long periods—forty to sixty minutes. Again, I felt lucky that he nursed so well and so often, and as a result I produced lots of milk. I wasn't yet aware of that crucial concept of a feedback loop for producing breastmilk: demand (nursing) and supply (making milk). At the time, I truly had no idea what I was doing with breastfeeding and was thankful that it worked for us.

I remember my mother having a theory that David would sleep through the night at six weeks of age if she fed him a large bottle of formula. One evening, she was babysitting, and after Phillip and I returned home from a date night, she happily announced, "He took a full bottle." David woke up three hours later, around 2 a.m., as usual. Sadly, he busted her theory; moreover, he didn't sleep through the night for five more weeks. My mother did not know that sleeping through the night is a brain thing and not a hunger thing. A few days later, I asked my husband to hint to my mother that she might refrain from giving me any more breastfeeding advice.

I needed Phillip to constantly reassure me and tell me that everything about our son seemed normal. Here I was—a double board-certified pediatrician and neonatologist—and I needed encouragement from my husband. Today, I understand that most new moms need this sort of reassurance. My initial lack of confidence was normal, even for a pediatrician mother. Although I enjoyed maternity leave at home with my son, I remember thinking about returning to work, looking forward to it, when David was six or seven weeks old. I distinctly remember being bored. I loved caring for him, holding, rocking, and nursing him, but there was no challenge, no thought process there.

About six weeks after her daughter was born, my older daughter mentioned to me that she wanted to return to her work as a nurse in the pediatric intensive care unit. She wondered if that was a bad thing. I tried to reassure her as I recollected how a lot of working moms would rather work than stay home full time with babies. Maybe it has to do with keeping busy. Maybe it's maternal style. Some women clearly crave the satisfaction and success from working. I've read that your personality type may play a role: Extroverted thinkers, as opposed to introverted feelers, tend not to stay at home with children. Regardless, some of us are just not meant to be stay-at-home mothers.

I was successful at breastfeeding my son—but only for about ten weeks. Once I was back at work full time, my breastfeeding became a failure and I felt defeated. As my busy days back in the NICU progressed, I'd slip away from the NICU to pump, but would produce less and less breastmilk. That was very discouraging, as I was unaware that I was not pumping often enough, and I was using a lousy breast pump, expressing milk from each breast separately for fifteen minutes at a time. In addition, I felt ambivalent about all the time it took to pump—more than thirty-five minutes away from the NICU. The maternal failure that I felt as my milk supply dwindled was profound, as if I had let my baby down. My feelings were all a jumble. I wanted to feed him in the best way possible, but I could not make it work long term. This was my earliest inclination that my two roles—physician and mother—were already in conflict.

I learned to deal with childcare issues—nannies and babysitters, on the fly. We were fortunate enough to afford a stay-at-home nanny and housekeeper. So many parents these days cannot. We never employed a live-in helper, or an au pair, but a lot of my doctor friends did. Of course, you need a large house and an extra room to provide that kind of luxury support. We were opposed to leaving our baby in a childcare center. In an effort to lessen his exposure to infectious diseases, we chose to have someone come to our home and stay with David during the day. The nanny would then leave once one of us got home.

I had an older neonatology friend and mentor, Reba, who advised me early on to pay my nanny legally. By that she meant to report to the state and federal government accurate data about the nanny's income and to withhold the appropriate amount of federal income and social security taxes. Several of my friends paid their caregivers cash under the table, but I was scared to do anything like that, something illegal.

For the first six months after David's birth, I continued to adjust to my working mother routine, and to my nanny, Mable. She was an elderly African American woman with years of childcare experience. She was sweet and quiet and oh-so-wonderful with my baby. She kept him bathed, dressed, and entertained. She played music for him, took him for walks in the stroller, and when he was asleep, she did laundry for us. Throughout my first two weeks back to work, she waited on me to return home at the end of each long day so that I could breastfeed him. However, the very next week she scolded me when I returned home after six p.m. several nights in a row. "He needs you more than this," she said. I have never forgotten those exact words, as it seems now such a testimony to the paradox faced by every working mother. Back in the NICU, I reverted quickly to working diligently and devoting my time to taking the best care of my patients. In doing so, I not only put off pumping but also put off leaving the hospital to get home on time.

Within my first motherhood tenure, I quickly realized that without a nanny (and housekeeper), I would not have been successful in practicing medicine. The same went for my husband. When I was absent, in the hospital on call at night, he did everything for our son. David was still an infant as I began to understand just how much of a trade-off working full time actually was, and I learned early on that working mothers carry guilt. My friends all had it too. Like most new mothers, I wanted to be a perfect mother, however I discovered at age thirty-four that there was so much I did not know or understand about babies. Imagine that—a neonatologist still learning about babies.

I also discovered early on that I could not accomplish everything by myself. Learning to engage my physician husband in childcare needs, especially when

David was sick, was problematic. When I called him in as a consultant, he was helpful. I told him that we had a problem and I asked him to help me solve it. Nevertheless, leaving a sick child at home with another caregiver and going into the NICU to make rounds was torture—my initial distressing experience with maternal guilt.

Reba had told me that she and her physician husband always employed two nannies (one for the weekends). And she reported that they often struggled like "ships passing in the night" raising their three girls. She described one of them heading home in response to a sick child or something going wrong. And then the other would drive home later to relieve the first one, and the cycle would continue. One day when David was about nine months old, Mable called to tell me that he had tumbled down the stairs and as a result got a large black-and-blue, goose-egg-sized lump on his forehead. Of course, I imagined that he had a skull fracture and rushed home to check on him. My husband headed home three hours later, so that I could return to the NICU to finish my work. This was our first rendition of "ships passing in the night" during those early years, and many others followed.

Another remarkable moment that stuck vividly in my mind occurred one morning when David was sick with a childhood virus or ear infection. He was about twelve months old and had awakened with a 102-degree fever. After treating his fever and dressing for work, I fixed us some breakfast and called the pediatrician's on-call service to set up an appointment. Shortly thereafter, I observed my husband straightening his tie, putting on his white coat, and heading out the front door. "Wait a minute, where are you going?" I asked him. "I'm going to work," he said. When I asked him, "What about David, what about me?" he said, "You'll take care of it. You always do." Then he turned and walked out the door, seemingly without a care. He apparently felt no guilt; he wasn't worried. He fully expected me to take care of everything, like I always did.

During my earliest years as a mother, there was a popular concept of a superwoman: TV ads in the 1980s told us that we could "bring home the bacon and fry it up in a pan." Working mothers were expected to do it all. My doctor friends and I all thought that we could be a supermom. What they did not tell us was that doctoring and mothering were both daunting, and each in different ways. They did not tell us that our children would need things from us at the most inopportune times, usually when work demanded our attention. I spent the first ten years of my own motherhood experience learning that there is no such thing as a "supermom." I came to understand that I was a typical working mother—constantly trying to balance full-time work and motherhood. Sometimes things were manageable, but often everything felt totally off balance and out of whack.

I hadn't entered the field of medicine to work part time. The training had been too long and arduous. Besides, I loved being a doctor. Medicine gave me a huge sense of contentment and competence. On balance, I loved practicing medicine as much as I loved being a mother. Caring for babies who were critically ill, watching them get better, and recover after a serious illness was extremely gratifying. Witnessing weak premature babies grow and thrive was rewarding. My two loves—neonatal medicine and motherhood—despite sounding similar, were different, and each filled up a different part of me.

NICU care in those days dealt commonly with one of the worst scourges in neonatal medicine: Group B Streptococcal infection. This was a bacterium commonly carried in a mother's vagina, generally not causing any maternal symptoms, but colonizing babies going through the birth canal. Babies infected with Group B Strep developed pneumonia, sepsis (bloodstream infection), septic shock, meningitis (infection around the brain), and even death. This was a bacterium that caused infants to collapse into shock when they were one or two days old, unless the mother first presented with prolonged rupture of membranes or fever. Those were some of the early warning signs alerting us to an infant at high risk for infection, so treatment could be started sooner.

Here was a typical scenario. You would enter the hospital room of a new mother to see her one-day-old infant who was said to be "grunting," making a soft, expiratory noise, a nonspecific sign of stress. You washed your hands, stood over the crib, pulled back the blanket, and you found a blue-gray newborn barely breathing with faint pulses. This extreme presentation was not uncommon, and this was the dreadful way babies with Group B Strep septic shock presented when I was a young attending. Group B Strep was a horrible infection, and despite antibiotic treatment, nearly fifty percent of infants who developed septic shock or meningitis died.

One of our NICU nurses, whom I knew well, delivered a full-term baby who seemed fine until he "crashed" at twenty-four hours of age. Her baby presented with full-blown Group B Strep septic shock. We resuscitated him one Saturday morning, placed him on a ventilator, gave him the fluids and medicines he needed, and hoped for the best. As usual, his infection was so overwhelming that our intensive care techniques made little difference, and tragically, this nurse's baby died the next day. This was my very first experience of informing parents of their baby's death. I will never forget sitting in mom's hospital room, giving her and her husband the horrible news as all three of us cried. That evening after I returned home, I picked up my sleeping infant son, hugged him, and cried some more. At the same time, I felt grateful that we had escaped this tragedy—such a mix of emotions. Unfortunately, I would see many other babies die from Group B Strep disease during my early years practicing in the NICU.

My life as a neonatologist and a working mother proceeded, and I continued to learn many new things as I went along those first two years. One Saturday morning post-call, I had been awake continuously for over twenty-four hours. My NICU shift had been long and difficult. The previous night we admitted fragile, 28 weeks gestation, premature twins, followed by yet another baby with Group B Strep sepsis. After checking out with my partner, I trudged home late that morning. Phillip was walking out the door on his way into the hospital to see his patients, and I was home alone with David, who was then a toddler. I was exhausted from my previous shift, but I attempted to play with my son for a while. I intended to play a little, then quickly put him down for a nap, but David had a different idea. He remained wide awake, eager to play, or read, or run around, or do anything other than sleep. I tried several times to make him lie down for his nap so that I could get some sleep.

Usually he was so easy to put down for a nap, but not that day. Every time I put him down in his crib, he popped up, fussing. Of course, this prevented me from getting my much-needed nap. This back and forth went on several times, and I just could not make him settle down and be quiet. My very short, frazzled fuse had been lit and I yelled at him. Then he began to cry. It pains me to admit that I found myself slapping his little legs, hard, over and over again. I was horrified, and I felt as if I had entered a dream. Somehow, I was able to go outside of myself and see what I was doing. I was slapping my helpless, beloved, little boy. This moment was so terrifying for me that I will never forget it. I had put red marks, handprints, on his little legs. My old childhood tapes had taken over playing in my brain. Fortunately, I recognized immediately that I was hurting him, stopped slapping him, grabbed and hugged him tightly. By then, both of us were crying fiercely. I sat down in the rocker and held him. Each of us cried for some time that day while I rocked him to sleep.

I did not want to let go of my son that day. I could hardly believe what I had done, but I knew that I needed help. On Monday I scheduled a visit with a psychologist. This woman helped me to see that I was programmed from an early age to react physically, like my father. She helped me understand that I knew well how to hit or slap, and scream, and yell. I had been raised in a household where screaming, yelling, and physical trauma were tolerated. It took some months, but she convinced me that I could learn a new way to be a mother, a way that did not involve any physical punishment. I desperately wanted to raise my children differently than my parents had raised me. I desperately wanted my children to know love, to feel like they were loved, and to grow up with good self-esteem.

So, I met with the psychologist regularly and persuaded my husband to join us, too. I needed him to assist me from boiling over when I was extremely tired or angry. Fortunately, that was the only incident throughout the first decade of my being a mother that I completely lost control of myself and hit my child. There were plenty of other times that I yelled or screamed at one of my children. Nevertheless, my singular goal for those early years was no hitting or slapping. In Houston, I slowly learned how to control myself with an active, small child and tolerate the stresses of full-time NICU work.

Chapter 4

BEGINNING

I was raised in Spartanburg, South Carolina, in the 1950s and 1960s. It was a typical Southern town, made up of mostly white, working-class people. Everyone, it seemed, attended church on Sundays. The Baptists went on Wednesdays, too. The public schools must have been adequate since I am a product of them. However, there was no integration until high school, so I went to public schools in segregated white neighborhoods. My own neighborhood nexus was a peaceful, dead-end street overflowing with children. It was a beautiful woodsy area that provided ample freedom. The seasons were lovely in South Carolina. Because my mother had a wonderful green thumb and always worked in our yard, everything around our one-story, ranch-style house appeared orderly and well-kept. Mother's flower beds were gorgeous, blooming during three seasons, and dainty dogwood trees blossomed all around. We had vividly colored autumn leaves in the fall, and in winter it snowed occasionally, which allowed for sledding, snow forts, and snowmen.

The outdoors in my neighborhood seemed limitless. All the front yards were deep and grassy, without fences between houses. Most of the backyards extended toward a creek. Trees for climbing were everywhere. Kids always seemed to be around; together, we rode bikes, skated, and played catch. For many years, it was a thrill to bike or sled down what we called "the big hill." We played Kick the Can, our favorite game, until dark forced us home. Softball was popular, too, and being a strong batter, I was always chosen for a team. Two quiet, shady creeks snaked through our neighborhood, providing the perfect places to sit alone, find attractive stones, or catch crawfish. We learned to watch out for water moccasins and to throw rocks to scare them away. We loved to wade up and down in Lawson's Fork Creek, the one that ran behind my house. Daddy fixed us a large rope swing with a big knot in the end. The bigger boys would bravely swing out and drop into the water, but most of us grabbed onto the rope, sat down, and swung out and back over the wide, shallow creek. In the Boyd's huge, woodsy backyard, we built elaborate tent cities in the spring and summer by stringing up blankets between trees. We raked neat pathways between the tents and placed rocks along the edges of the paths. Many hours were consumed pretending and playing outside with friends in the shade of our tents.

My sister, Marianne, and I shared a bedroom for many years. Both of my brothers had their own rooms. My sister was sixteen months my junior and we argued and fought quite a lot. She was my mother's favorite and that made me mad. Plus, she was blonde and very pretty. Smaller than me, she had dreamy, soft, blue eyes and a wistful, innocent look. She remembered that I picked on her mercilessly. My father usually broke up our fights, and when he did, he inevitably blamed me. I was an argumentative and bossy child and fought with my best friend who lived next door. In elementary school I was often required to sit outside of the classroom for talking too much or made to sit right next to the teacher's desk at the front of the classroom. This was embarrassing but did not curtail my talking. It seems like I was always in trouble in grade school.

As a young child, my hair was curly and the color of a copper penny. It must have looked a mess since I was a tomboy. People always commented on my hair, and they insisted on touching it. They all loved my hair, but it made me feel like an anomaly who never fit in. The other kids in my neighborhood called me names, like "red strings" and "carrot top." Plenty of adults happily called me "carrot top," too. As the years passed by, my hair became a rich auburn color. It remained curly, and often frizzy. That was a problem during the 1960s, a time when straight, long blonde hair was the trend. My friends helped me iron my hair when I was in high school. That was a real feat, and we all endured some finger burns.

My father was a harsh disciplinarian. He joined the Navy at age eighteen and served in World War II as a medic in the South Pacific. He must have witnessed many dreadful things in the war; nevertheless, he continued to serve in the Navy Reserve for many more years. Daddy was extremely strict and often lost control of his temper. He whipped us all with his belt, especially me. I remember running down the hall trying to escape, the belt strap stinging my legs. That strap made long, red welts on my skin. Once, he lined up all four of us—my siblings and me—and made us stand at attention. After screaming at us, he slapped my face and pulled my hair. My mother was somewhere nearby, watching and saying nothing. She must have feared him, too. Daddy yelled at my baby brother, Bennett, so often. Bennett was a sensitive, little, red-headed kid. Once, I witnessed Daddy scream at him because he kept crying after running home with a deep cut in his knee. He was only five or six years old, and his knee was actively bleeding. Daddy did not comfort, only screamed.

One day, after spending a long weekend at my grandfather's farm, my mother was driving us home from Greensboro. We were late because of a flat tire along the way. Mother pulled over so that my older brother, Ted, could change it. My father waited over an hour for us to get home and must have been worried that we had all been hurt. But when we finally arrived, he screamed at my mother for being late and not telling him. She calmly explained everything that had happened, yet he balled up his fist, hit her hard in the mouth, and busted her lip. I was standing close by watching and screamed. Mother did not flinch but looked at me and spoke to him: "She will never forget this as long as she lives." She was right. My father lost control so easily, that, as a result, we were always jumpy around him. You never knew when he might blow up. Sometimes we needed to tiptoe around carefully. But worst of all: He never apologized for anything he did to us. Nothing. Ever.

Every Sunday morning, we all went to Trinity Methodist church as a family and pretended that everything was normal. This was after hearing my father scream at my sister for her habitual tardiness. My father volunteered as an usher, and both he and mother served on various church committees. My mother was a member of a circle of women who performed good deeds in the community. For many years, my father was the Boy Scout master at our church. Daddy's proudest moment occurred when Ted achieved Eagle Scout. He acted as if he had accomplished the honor himself. Daddy berated Bennett for dropping out of Scouts at the rank of Star.

Since my mother worked full time when I was in elementary school, we always had a maid. Mother's maids were African American and poor. Gertrude lived in the low-income apartment projects across town and worked for my mother for over ten years. She was a large, kind, and jolly woman, and she was a fabulous cook. My brother, Ted, was her favorite, and she made him sweet cornbread muffins whenever he asked for them. I have an endearing photograph of Gertrude with me when I was a child; in it, we're standing in front of our house, and she's holding my hand. She had fixed my hair nicely with a large blue bow to match my dress. Later, Hannah worked for Mother. She was tall and thin, a quiet and reserved woman. Hannah appeared a little scary because she had one deformed eye that had been damaged years before by cleaning fluid. But she was always nice to us. Sometimes, at the end of a long day, my mother drove her home to her small house far outside of town. Her house looked to me like a shack. These nice women were not nannies. They cleaned house, did laundry and ironing, did some cooking, fed us snacks, and watched after us. They did not help with homework and did not drive us anywhere.

In Mrs. Kingman's sixth-grade class, I learned that making good grades garnered some positive attention from my parents. Mrs. Kingman was an attractive, energetic redhead, and a great teacher. Under her watchful eye, it was easy to become a good student by always reading and doing homework. Mrs. Kingman bestowed upon me extra reading material, and Mother brought home many classics from the elementary school where she was the librarian. By junior high school, I made all As, except I didn't take Latin, like the smartest kids.

When my older brother went off to college, Daddy gave him a GTO, an expensive, manly car. I was glad to get Ted's old Ford Falcon with the manual stick shift. I started driving at age fourteen, the legal age back then, and I delighted in giving other kids rides to and from school. One time in ninth grade, however,

I borrowed Mother's station wagon to drive a carload of teenagers home. It was a rainy afternoon, and I turned too quickly. I lost control of the car, swerved and hit a parked car, plowed onto the other side of the street, and knocked over a bookmobile parked behind the public library. Only then did Mother's wagon come to a stop. Unbelievably, no one was hurt. My wreck made the front page of our town's newspaper: "Three Teens Injured." I don't recall my parents being upset about this; maybe I was in shock and nothing they said registered. Nevertheless, they allowed me to keep driving, and I didn't have another wreck until my late twenties.

Lagging behind my peers in pubertal development was emotional torture. Not only was my younger sister prettier than me, but also, she started her period and grew boobs before me. But she wasn't a good student, didn't care much about school, and made mostly Cs. I didn't start my period until I was sixteen. That felt abnormal and confusing. Around that same time, I began to have acne—the bad, cystic kind. My mother took me to the dermatologist, who opened and drained my biggest pimples and set me under a sunlamp until I burned slightly. Unfortunately, there were few effective treatments for acne at that time. Traipsing back and forth to the dermatologist and smearing various creams on my face didn't help. I felt like a freak with tender, red bumps surmounted by pustules scattered over my face. Teenagers with cystic acne always look so wounded, and I felt that way, too. My cystic acne continued throughout most of high school. It wasn't until someone put me on a high-dose estrogen birth-control pill that the pimples subsided, but a lot of facial scars were left behind. Acne is hardly a life-threatening disease, but it is certainly a life-altering disease.

Although I wanted to, I didn't date boys in high school. My friends all did, so I lived vicariously through them. My three best friends, Alice, Martha, and Louise were two pretty blondes and a brunette. All three had long straight hair that curled attractively after applying rollers. Each had clear skin and nice figures. Each attended every dance, prom, and homecoming. My friends were average students, so we gathered often for study sessions and did homework together. Two of my girlfriends had moms who smoked, so our clique began smoking cigarettes in the eleventh grade. Alice and I used to drive to the library and the Hardee's hamburger joint to look for boys and smoke cigarettes. I thought I could hide this new development from my parents, but of course, they caught me smoking and were furious. That didn't stop me from smoking.

I also kept studying and reading. I made straight As in high school and discovered that I liked math, chemistry, and biology. Making As continued to bring positive attention from my parents. They complimented my grades and praised my efforts, but we never talked about my feelings of marginalization because of having acne and not dating. My mother never talked to me about boys. Two of the girls who lived on my street were debutantes. Their fathers were businessmen and their mothers came from Virginia. Other girls I knew, whose fathers were doctors or lawyers, also "came out" during high school, a clear demonstration of the power of the upper class in my hometown. My family was middle class, and so, this custom was something I could not experience.

I had a most wonderful grandmother. My "Mamaw" was Daddy's mother, and I was her favorite. She lived in Baton Rouge and visiting her there was heavenly. Her big, shady yard had fig and persimmon trees for climbing, camellia bushes for picking pretty, fragrant blossoms, and neighborhood streets perfect for biking. Her kitchen, located in the back of her old house, was filled with smells of French drip coffee and a fresh pot of grits—creamy, buttery, thick and delicious. In the summer, Mamaw always invited me along on Trailways' bus trips with her lady friends. They traveled together around the states and visited many national parks. I experienced Yellowstone, Jackson Hole, Carlsbad Caverns, Mount Rushmore, and other spectacular places with her. My Mamaw made me feel special, and she never fussed at me. When I was younger, she mailed my sister and me boxes filled with Easter hats and gloves. She always sent sweet cards with quarters taped inside. When I was older, she mailed dollar bills to me inside cards and letters. She even hand-embroidered towels with my initials for my first apartment. Throughout high school and college, Mamaw wrote me many long letters in her lovely, cursive handwriting.

I loved my Mamaw dearly and regret not being able to see her before her death. Although I visited her briefly when she became ill with pancreatic cancer, I was unable to say a final goodbye. (My parents did not inform me of her death for several days because "they did not want to upset me" during med school.) I discovered much later in my adult life that my beloved Mamaw had sent away my father and his younger brother—they were eight and six—to live with their Aunt Cora and Uncle Benny. Even though she was a devout Catholic, Mamaw was divorcing their father. She told me that he was extremely jealous and possessive, but I don't know if he hurt her physically. So, Daddy and his brother lived with their aunt and uncle for two years, and I am convinced that the abandonment by his mother played a role in my father's anger issues. Mamaw told me once that she was nicest to me because my father was hardest on me.

My little sister, Marianne, not only made average grades, but also hung out with some "bad boys" from the wrong side of town. She got pregnant at fourteen and tearfully approached me about her predicament. I will never forget the shock of that moment as we stood together in our bathroom. She was pregnant—and I had not even started my period. Having no idea how to help her, I forced her to walk into our parents' bedroom and report the awful news. My mother remained calm and speechless. My father screamed and called her a slut and a whore. Mother arranged to take Marianne to New York City to have an abortion. They were gone for two days, and nothing more was ever said about her becoming pregnant or having an abortion. Saying nothing was my family's approach to dealing with significant trauma.

Marianne and I shared only a few positive childhood memories. In the winter, we liked to lie on our backs, put our feet up on the hearth, and warm our toes in front of the fireplace. We had fun building tents in our bedroom, and we loved sledding together. On Sunday afternoons, we listened to West Side Story and other splendid albums while lounging in the living room. We learned to dance together in 1960 listening to Chubby Checker's "The Twist."

In 1969, after high school graduation, I began college at Auburn University in the sleepy town of Auburn, Alabama. It was entertaining to live in a dorm for two years with some feisty, pretty girls who became my sorority sisters. Chris and Cathy came from Atlanta and Birmingham. Our time together was always spirited and fun, and I began to date. The fraternity houses had great parties, and we danced to soul music and Creedence Clearwater Revival. We drank beer and Purple Passion. A few people smoked grass. I tried it once but didn't like the way it made me feel. My first year in college, I didn't study much, and my grades were just average, the result of too much partying.

It amuses me now that an aptitude test I took at Auburn in 1971 indicated that I was well suited to be a social worker or a physical education teacher. Nevertheless, during my sophomore year, I settled down and focused on getting into medical school. Over the previous summer, I clerked in my hometown hospital's medical records department. Elizabeth, an articulate and expressive records manager, was encouraging. She was an energetic, short, Lebanese dynamo, and her staff loved her intensity and know-how. She befriended me that summer and allowed me to accompany her to lunches in the hospital cafeteria and various medical staff meetings. Babysitting her two children that summer was enjoyable, and during that period, she convinced me that I could do whatever I wanted.

Early in my junior year, I moved into an apartment off campus with my two best friends, Chris and Cathy. We lived there for the last two years of college. In that tiny two-bedroom apartment, we cooked and talked, sang and danced, and had wonderful times. We were delighted by beach house parties on the Alabama Gulf Coast during spring break and sorority formal dances in large hotels in Atlanta. Carole King's "Tapestry" and "Bye, Bye Miss American Pie" were the soundtracks of my last college years. Because it was noisy in our apartment, I frequently excused myself to go study with Daniel and Ray, two guys who were also premed. We studied together four nights a week, and I worshiped being their sidekick. Whenever I needed to, I took Eskatrol, an amphetamine diet pill, to stay awake all night and study for big tests. Afterwards, my sleep was reclaimed with long naps the next day. You could buy these pills from the fraternity boys for two or three dollars each. Somehow, the boys got the pills from the doctor at the campus health clinic. This drug was taken off the market in 1981 because the manufacturer was unable to prove the drug's effectiveness as a weight-loss agent. At that time, however, it was among the hundred most prescribed drugs in the United States.

I took physical chemistry the summer between my junior and senior years. The P chem lab experiments confounded me. I worked hard, but the course was so tough that I made a C. That course was known to be difficult for even the smartest chemistry geeks. Nevertheless, this sweet, older P chem professor was understanding. His warm smile, his everyday outfit of black pants, a dingy white shirt and skinny black tie, and his large hands, dusty with chalk, are unforgettable.

He gave me a B when he heard I wanted to be a doctor. And thanks to him, I majored in both biology and chemistry and ended up with a GPA high enough for medical school admission. Then, in my senior year in college, I was proud to make the Mortar Board society, which was a huge honor. There were only twenty of us chosen at Auburn that year. Unbelievably, my parents surprised me and showed up for my induction ceremony. This was the only time they had visited me at college since dropping me off at the start of freshman year.

My parents paid for my college education and for all my sorority fees. So, perhaps my mother did, in fact, want me to have a good time at Auburn. I desperately wanted to go to the University of Alabama Medical School, where my two premed friends planned to attend. Sadly, I was not accepted there, despite having a 3.67 GPA and good MCAT scores. This was a huge disappointment; however, I was accepted to the Medical University of South Carolina in Charleston. So, in 1973 I headed back to my home state for medical school.

Chapter 5

MATERNAL GIFTS

From the beginning of my career, I received profound gifts from special people—extraordinary parents who settled close by my sickest patients and slowly revealed themselves to me. Beatrice was one of those exceptional mothers. One night when I was on call, she was the high-risk pregnant woman who was transferred into our L&D. She was a PhD psychologist with premature rupture of membranes, pregnant with extremely premature twins at 24 weeks gestation. Hers were invitro fertilization (IVF) babies, and the year was 1985. After briefly meeting her and her husband, I attended her delivery. At birth, each of her babies weighed less than one pound five ounces. Both little girls were quickly placed on ventilatory support and whisked away to the NICU. We inserted catheters into their umbilicus (belly button) to provide fluids and nutrition, and to monitor lab values, and then we covered them with Saran wrap plastic blankets to prevent heat and fluid loss.

Twin A was much sicker than her sister because of severe pneumonia and sepsis (a blood stream infection). She had white blood cell counts that were markedly abnormal and blood pressure that was too low. She looked dusky and pale and was also minimally responsive. From the start, twin B was more stable and settled into her new environment on lower ventilator settings. She had bright red, thin skin, downy hair on her wrinkled forehead, barely visible blonde eyebrows, and fused eyelids. Her nose and lips were perfectly formed, but her ears were floppy and folded in on themselves, sticking to her scalp. Her head seemed disproportionately large for her scrawny body. She had tiny fingers with barely visible nails, and veins could be seen beneath her translucent skin all over her body. Twin B looked decent for 24 weeks gestation, and she did not appear to have active infection, although we treated her with the same antibiotics regardless.

I dutifully updated the girls' parents in mother's room that first night, explained their situations, and tried to describe how critically unstable twin A was. They were shocked but expressed appreciation for all our efforts to save their twins. I knew that most parents in this situation were terrified and overwhelmed. Updating parents after delivery is crucial, though, especially if the mother has been unable to physically see her babies. These updates to parents about their babies during their first hours were routine procedures for us, yet vitally important for new parents of extremely premature infants. I attempted to cautiously estimate each girl's chances of survival and briefly described the treatments each received. I knew that too much information was unlikely to be retained. Like other IVF parents, this couple seemed desperate for these little girls. Typically, most IVF parents act this way since they have been through so much to conceive and carry their babies.

Twin B remained stable, furrowed her brow, and squirmed around in response to stimulation, while her sister deteriorated throughout their first day. Twin A continued to languish and died on her second day of life. I disliked giving her parents this news. This was not my first instance of relaying such terrible news, but each time I did, it disturbed me. After five years practicing in the NICU, it was no less depressing to witness a baby die, even a very immature infant with overwhelming sepsis (who was never really expected to survive). Later that day, her blood cultures turned positive for Group B Streptococcus, so I rationalized that my explaining the reason for the girls' premature delivery and twin A's rapid demise somehow made it more tolerable for their parents. Knowing the reason for death does not diminish their loss but does provide closure for some parents.

Of course, these parents were extremely sad to lose one daughter, but seemed optimistic about twin B, who they named Janie.

The surviving sister turned out to be a little fighter and was unusually active and responsive for a preemie at 24 weeks gestation. She often wiggled around in her warming bed and seemed to enjoy sucking on her miniature pacifier. As her ventilator settings were weaned down, I began to feel optimistic about her chances and continued to update her parents every day. Janie continued to do well and was tolerating small feedings, drops of her mother's breastmilk, until she developed a patent ductus arteriosus, or PDA. This is a common complication of prematurity, a blood vessel opening near the heart that floods the lungs with blood. It is treated with a medicine called indomethacin that usually closes the open ductus. I explained the risks and benefits to her mother, and she agreed to the treatment.

Regrettably, several doses of the medicine did not work on Janie, and because her PDA continued to flood her lungs with blood, she needed a surgical ligation, or tying off, of her PDA. As her parents adjusted to the new PDA diagnosis and her need for urgent surgery, I grew to like them for their constant, calm presence and their positivity. This little baby's mother sat by her bedside with a hand gently resting on her daughter's arm or leg throughout most of every day. The surgical procedure, a thoracotomy (open chest procedure) and PDA ligation, was performed in the NICU and was successful. After surgery, Janie grew stronger, tolerated her feedings, and again began to wean off her vent settings.

Dad returned to work, but Janie's mom remained nearby each day. She was always in the NICU, sitting at her bedside. We talked every day about her daughter's labs, her exams, and her progress. At three weeks of age, when she was almost ready to come off the ventilator, she took a turn for the worse and developed pneumonia. That caused her to retreat to higher oxygen and vent settings for support. I felt discouraged with this complication, even though I knew that many small babies on ventilators developed pneumonia as a complication of prolonged ventilation. But this time I allowed her mother to see my disappointment. I remember not wanting to give her false hope since we were dealing with yet another complication requiring more medications. Nevertheless, her mother remained optimistic. Janie was one of my sickest NICU patients, but there were twelve other babies in the unit that I cared for daily during that time as well. I worked diligently in the NICU and cared for each of my small charges and updated their parents daily. I enjoyed using my skills and my growing competency, and I especially liked my job as a young neonatologist.

Again, I never entered the field of medicine to work part time. The training had been prolonged and too difficult, and I really loved being a doctor. Despite being raised in the 1950s in South Carolina, when most women stayed at home, my role model—my own mother—was a working mother. Armed with a master's degree, she worked full time as an elementary school librarian. In addition, she was often away from home doing volunteer work for our church. She was a respected leader in her community of librarians, teachers, and church groups, displaying her own style of super-mom during that era. When she came home after a long school day, she prepared dinner for her family of six. Just like me, my mother always needed help, and that was provided by caring and quiet African-American maids. They looked after us when she was away at her school, and they cleaned house and did laundry. She treated them kindly and, I presume, paid them fairly.

As our son, David, quickly grew those first two years, I continued to learn that there is no such thing as a "super-mom." I was absent from him too much, working most days and taking night call in the hospital. I know now that no full-time working mother can be gone more than forty hours each week and really know everything that is going on with her child. I felt extremely lucky to have married another pediatrician, since he was there when I was gone. His call schedule was lighter than mine, and our trade-off for that was his doing most of the cooking. Phillip was especially calm when things went awry but never seemed as hungry for knowledge as me. I consumed stacks of books written by experts on child behavior and child development. (Thank goodness there was no internet back then, or I would have been addicted.) I needed to know if all the things I observed with my son were normal. As it turned out, David demonstrated several childhood conditions that I neither encountered nor learned about in my own pediatric training.

Night terrors stumped me first as a new mother. I was terrified when I first witnessed them. A night terror looks like your child is possessed by some demon.

David developed them suddenly around eighteen months of age, and I had no idea what they were. Night terrors occur most often in toddlers and preschoolers and take place during deep sleep. During a night terror, your child cries uncontrollably, has a terrified, confused, or glassy-eyed look, screams, kicks, or stares and does not recognize you or realize you are there. You cannot wake your child up, or calm him down, or even soothe him. You must let the night terror run its course. Fortunately, unlike nightmares, the child does not remember the episode the next day. Thankfully, these terrifying episodes resolved over the next few months.

Back in the world of NICU work, Janie, my favorite preemie, stayed in the NICU for four more months. After her pneumonia was treated and she stabilized, her mother asked me one day, "Is she going to make it?" Standing at her bedside, I paused and took a slow, deep breath. Then I answered, "Probably. Most preemies as small as she is who survive for the first month tend to survive overall." Mom nodded her head in understanding, even as I reminded her that she still had much to overcome. In anticipation, we talked about her developing chronic lung disease, or bronchopulmonary dysplasia, a typical complication of small premature babies who were supported on oxygen and a ventilator during their first month of life. We also talked about the possibility of other infections, and her mother listened carefully.

At six weeks of age, Janie developed early signs of retinopathy of prematurity, or ROP, another complication of prematurity, one related to immature retinae and oxygen exposure. At that time, her mother consented to allow her baby to participate in a clinical study of vitamin E, an antioxidant, given to prevent severe ROP. Janie's ROP progressed to a severe stage, however, and at eight weeks of age she required cryosurgery on her retinae, a procedure to prevent retinal detachment. Thank goodness, her ROP stabilized and her retinas did not detach—she did not go blind. (But Janie would end up with poor vision and wear Coke-bottle-thick glasses for a long time before she could be fitted with contact lenses at age three.)

Because her mother was so nice and pleasant, I enjoyed caring for Janie, even though the baby herself was problematic. Some NICU moms were, understandably, not warm about anything, and that made my work with their babies and my tedious explanations that much more difficult. Janie slowly weaned off the ventilator during her third and fourth months, and when she was at a corrected age of 40 weeks gestation, essentially full-term, she was ready to be taken off the vent, or extubated. That morning, both mom and I were excited, almost giddy, to see her finally extubated. We were both relieved that she tolerated extubation well. However, a few days later, I noticed her hoarse cry. I felt disheartened, knowing what the problem was, and dreaded having to explain to her mother that one of her vocal cords was paralyzed, most likely the result of the earlier PDA surgery.

Janie also developed some rib fractures resulting from poor bone mineralization. Back then, we were still learning how to properly use mothers' own breastmilk for adequate nutrition in extremely small preterm babies. Because of the milk's inherently low protein levels, and less than adequate milk fortifiers available at that time, Janie, being fed exclusively her mother's milk, received inadequate protein, calcium, and phosphorus intake, and grew more slowly than expected. In addition, the diuretic medicines that we typically gave babies with chronic lung disease caused calcium wasting into her urine. Again, her mother agreed unselfishly to enroll her daughter into a clinical trial of bone density and breastmilk feedings that was being conducted at TCH at the time.

Although her daughter suffered through many complications, severe chronic lung disease and retinopathy of prematurity, and while I cared for her through all of this and two surgeries, Beatrice was always pleasant and extremely tolerant of her daughter's ups and downs. She had a smile for everyone and often complimented the nurses' work. She listened carefully and asked a lot of questions. Perhaps she was analyzing all of us. More likely she was just being present for her daughter and her caregivers. There were many days when something went wrong with her baby, and I felt defeated. Some days, when I felt discouraged and struggled to stay upbeat about her daughter, Beatrice kept a positive attitude and supported me.

There was never a time that I did not enjoy talking with Janie's mom, and over all those months in the NICU, I grew fond of both her and her daughter. Throughout Janie's NICU stay, Beatrice became attached to two physicians—the one conducting the bone density study, and me. The three of us each shared a vision of Janie as our personal triumph. She had survived everything her young life threw at her. It is somewhat unusual, but also a great honor, to connect so deeply with one particular mother in the NICU.

Long after Janie had been discharged home, her mom kept in touch with me by sending little notes and pictures of her daughter. When I moved away from Houston, she continued to update me. They visited me once while I was living in Little Rock in the early 1990s. And after I moved to Austin many years later, this clever and committed mother located me so that she could reintroduce me to her grown daughter. We met at a nearby hamburger joint in Austin.

Janie had played trumpet in her high school band. Even though she had a scratchy, hoarse voice, she was incredibly talented with the trumpet. The year her mom found me, Janie entered the University of Texas at Austin as a freshman. She did well in school there, loved playing in the Longhorn Band for three years, and she learned fencing épée, a complicated and challenging sport. She graduated in 2009 with a degree in Radio, TV, and Film. Her mother was every bit as delighted and proud of her daughter then as she had been during the first week after birth, and through all her travails.

Janie's mom went on to volunteer with Child Protective Services for many years in Liberty, Texas, where she lived and worked as a clinical psychologist. Recently, I questioned her about whether her daughter's personality might have been affected by all the NICU pain that she endured. She reminisced that as she witnessed the invasiveness of the tests and support that kept Janie alive in the NICU, she wondered even then what the ramifications of those experiences would be. She remembered that "while the 'mother' side of her rejoiced that she was still alive day after day, the 'psychologist' side of her—acutely aware that much of an individual's personality is formed during our earliest years—was worrying about what the effects would be." She told me, "I hoped my presence would help mitigate the painful experiences and tried to spend time by Janie's side every day and hold her tiny arm or leg until we were finally allowed to hold her (which was not until she was several weeks old)." I felt honored that Janie's mother shared not only her daughter, but also those intimate feelings with me.

Maternal strength of a different kind is illustrated by Jacob's story—a memorable one, not for his degree of prematurity or severity of illness, but for his parents' challenging situation. I encountered his parents one month before his birth, because his mother's obstetrician consulted me to counsel them. After my OB colleague called, I carefully checked current statistics before I approached the couple with some trepidation. We met in mother's hospital room since she was not in labor. She had just been diagnosed with stage two cervical cancer and was, at that time, pregnant with her son Jacob at 24 weeks gestation.

The husband, a bright and inquisitive chemical engineer, seemed nice, but drilled me with numerous questions about the outcomes of preterm babies born at various gestational ages between 24 and 30 weeks. He had already researched these data but listened and took notes from the information I presented. When mom asked, I gave her my usual spiel—that the best cutoff for normal outcomes was around 28 weeks gestation. Most babies born at that gestational age go on to become completely normal children. We discussed survival rates and possible outcomes for babies born at 24 to 28 weeks gestation. Obviously, the couple was struggling to decide whether to terminate the pregnancy, when to deliver their son, and when to start cancer treatment for his mother. (I learned much later that Jacob's mother desperately wanted to provide her husband with a legacy—the gift of a son.) The day after our meeting, I learned that the couple, with the guidance of her obstetrician, decided to wait another month to begin her cancer therapy.

So, Jacob was born one month later in August 1987, at 28 weeks gestation, weighing three pounds, four ounces. He entered the world with a robust cry and mature lungs—a big, healthy preemie. In the NICU, he had few problems and was relatively easy to care for. He had minimal apnea, no infections, and no complications. Jacob remained in the NICU for seven weeks and gained weight well. His father visited often, was continually curious, asked lots of questions, and always took copious notes. Meanwhile, his mother began her cancer treatment and, as a result, was often unable to visit. After delivery, she underwent a radical hysterectomy, which was followed by radiation therapy. Sometime later, she endured chemotherapy as well.

When I was not working in the NICU, I enjoyed my home life and began to appreciate it as a respite from the hospital. We lived in a small two-story house in Montrose, a quiet, mixed Houston neighborhood. Other young, professional families lived nearby, as did several gay couples, and middle-income Latino families lived in apartments in the area. A modest, shady park with a playground was close by. I enjoyed stroller rides around our friendly neighborhood sidewalks and into that little park.

Because I grew up in a small neighborhood, playing outside with other children until dark, I wanted that experience for my children. That time outside as a child felt to me like wonderful freedom. I imagined that our Houston neighborhood would be like that, one where all the mothers knew all the children. I also attended a nearby Methodist church, enjoyed my adult Sunday school class there, and was pleased that David liked attending his preschool class there two days a week.

David was a little over three years old when I encountered Jacob's parents again a year later. They joined the same Methodist church that I attended. At the time, Jacob's mother was pale, frail, and clearly struggling with painful, invasive cervical cancer. Her initial treatments failed, and she was slowly deteriorating. Tragically, she died when Jacob was only sixteen months old. This brave, young woman had been willing to sacrifice her own life to save her son's and to maximize his ultimate outcome. I wondered if I would have done the same thing. Her funeral service was held in our gorgeous cathedral sanctuary, and I remember sitting there sobbing, since her death seemed to me a heartbreaking loss. The associate pastor sitting next to me that day remarked that she "was sorry to see me in so much pain." It took me years to understand what she might have meant.

Jacob's father continued to attend my church, and we became friends. He and my husband got along well, since they were both bright, jovial, and sarcastic. My husband and I often met Jacob's dad as we gathered up our sons after church. We liked to go out all together for Sunday lunch and allow our boys to play. Jacob's dad was an attentive, loving father to his toddler, but he seemed lonely. After some time passed, he asked me to recommend someone for him to date. Fortunately, I had one single friend who worked as a PICU nurse and was smart, attractive, and outgoing. I introduced them, they dated, seemed well-suited, and enjoyed spending time together. They were married about a year later and continue to be happily married to this day, some thirty years later. Jacob was blessed with a new mother, and his father gained a healthy, loving wife.

His parents had another son soon thereafter to complete their family. I joyfully attended their new son's delivery, another milestone for their family. After all these years, that couple remains two of our best friends. I am delighted that I helped create such a perfect match and feel privileged to have participated in the metamorphosis of Jacob's family.

Despite my full-time work in the NICU, I tried to be an involved mother for my toddler son. That meant that I attempted to be present for his school events and tried to pick him up after preschool occasionally. But there is just no way on earth that one person can be in two places at once. Maybe if you are Hermione Granger in the Harry Potter books, but not if you are me. My favorite, yet horrible, early memory of this lesson was David's first Mother's Day tea, held at the church preschool. He was three years old, and I was held up leaving the hospital because one of my babies took a turn for the worse. That baby needed immediate attention. Ultimately, she needed intubation—a tube inserted into her airway—and because of my work ethic, I felt that I could not leave the situation to someone else. I paged my husband and begged him to attend the tea for me while I stayed to oversee the care and stabilization of that baby. I have the cutest picture of my husband receiving David's handmade Mother's Day artwork in my stead. The art was a small, purple, left handprint inked onto cloth, and Phillip is sitting in a little chair at a low, round table next to David, both drinking milk and eating a cookie. David was content; he didn't notice that my husband was the only father there. On the other hand, I felt miserable for days.

So, I continued to learn that working mothers carried guilt. My friends all had it, too. And as we compared notes on work and child-rearing, and our attempts to be involved in our children's lives, we began to understand just how much of a trade-off working full time really was. There were plenty of days when one could be an efficient, dedicated doctor, and other days when one could be an attentive, loving mother. Yet those days were rarely the same.

Chapter 6

PARENTAL INSPIRATION

O ur parents disciplined us differently than we intended to discipline our own children. Parents were more authoritative in the 1950s and '60s. The other neighborhood mothers would phone your mother if you acted up in their yard or home. My parents were strict. Daddy was a Navy man who survived World War II fighting in the South Pacific. He served as a medic and undoubtedly suffered some deep wounds from that experience, and he always needed to be correct. He often said, "Because I said so," and Daddy's rules were set without discussion. Mother grew up as an only child on a working farm. She remembered doing whatever chores she was told to do without question, so she always agreed with Daddy's rules and left the punishments up to him. (Much later, I began to wonder whether she had been hit by her father as a child, since she often stood by and watched my father hit us without intervening.)

My husband's father acted similarly in his family of origin—he used physical punishment and name-calling on many occasions. He was an oil field worker during the war, and later drove a milk delivery truck. My husband remembers being hit, pushed, or kicked by his father. Both of us remember the shame of being called names by our fathers when we were kids. Phillip and I discussed discipline before having children, and although we knew little about other methods, we planned to be lenient parents. From the outset, we both cared more about our children's self-esteem than setting limits or strict discipline. I wanted our children to grow up feeling loved and protected, and not in harm's way.

Once our second child came along two years after the first, I strived to understand and manage even more early childhood problems—breastfeeding difficulties, sibling rivalry, temper tantrums, toddler discipline, and what sort of preschool would best serve our children. Controlling sibling rivalry took great effort, more effort than my attempts to control some complication that one of my premature infants might develop. Neither rivalry nor an unwanted complication is entirely predictable, and both are difficult to tolerate.

When I visit with new mothers who have just delivered their second baby, we always discuss sibling rivalry. I predict that they will have far more trouble with the first child than they will with the new baby. In general, this is true if the first child is two to three years old when number two is born. But sibling rivalry can be normal at any age. Sometimes it starts even before the second child is born and continues as the children grow and compete for attention. As children reach different stages of development, their evolving needs affect how they relate to one another. David, the first-born son, was doted upon as an infant and toddler. He was bright, active, and musical, and he had grown accustomed to getting all our undivided attention.

When Anne came home from the hospital, he was only two and a half years old and was jealous immediately. He was a cute toddler with a thick mop of golden-brown hair, bright blue eyes, a sly smile, and a bouncy gait. I remember him walking around the nursery, newly decorated for a baby girl, and tapping his little plastic hammer on things as he walked around, as if he were keeping time to music. As he approached his new baby sister, he looked at her, glanced up at me, then wacked her on her forehead, hard enough to leave a red mark. Anne screamed a loud, painful wail. This was my earliest, startling confrontation with sibling rivalry. To this day, that instance continues to be a favorite story from our family lore. For the next few months David attempted to pinch, poke, prod, or hit Anne, and we could not leave him alone anywhere near his baby sister. Like many other toddlers, he acted out when I sat down to breastfeed his sister. He had some sense that I was distracted or, at the very least, unable to jump up and catch him doing something he knew better than to do. When I learned to hold a book and read it out loud and breastfeed at the same time, his rivalry and bad behavior settled down quite a bit.

Once when I was nursing Anne, David asked if he could breastfeed, as many young children do. When I let him, he did not suck, only licked my nipple. When he tasted some expressed breast milk, he announced, "It's sweet," and never again asked about or interfered with breastfeeding. A dear friend, also a pediatrician, gave me a terrific tip on how to be proactive in giving my son one-on-one attention. When he could keep it together and behave throughout the morning, I would take him outdoors for a walk or go to the park in the afternoon. A big reward for him was to sit and read together, just the two of us, once his father returned home from work to help with his baby sister.

In the early years of my career, mothering two small children and practicing at Texas Children's Hospital, I was graced by being able to take part in the care of many exceptional cases—ill babies and their parents. Working with these families contributed to my becoming an empathetic and thoughtful neonatologist. In 1988, when Anne was around one year old, I was called STAT to attend the delivery of Emily, a baby born with infantile polycystic kidney disease, or IPKD. I was summoned STAT to her delivery at St. Luke's Hospital, located adjacent to TCH. The pediatrician needed help with a newborn in severe respiratory distress. Emily was born to her lawyer mother and theoretical chemist father; she was a much wanted and planned pregnancy. Her older sister was seven years old. When I arrived, Emily was blue and struggling to breathe despite receiving some blow-by oxygen. After quickly examining her, I noted her squashed facial features, her bell-shaped thorax, her deep chest retractions, and her protuberant abdomen with easily palpable, large cystic kidneys. They felt like two huge, hard bunches of grapes. I told the pediatrician that she must have Potter's syndrome. He was doubtful, but to me all her features were indicative. In fact, she did prove to have infantile polycystic kidney disease, which presents with Potter's syndrome—the features described above. IPKD is a rare genetic disorder affecting one in 20,000 children.

After Emily was intubated, we transported her to the NICU, inserted bilateral chest tubes for her pneumothoraxes, and stabilized her on the ventilator. Pneumothorax occurs when perforation in the diseased lung allows air to trap between the lung and chest wall, causing compression of the lung. Thankfully, her pulmonary hypoplasia—lung underdevelopment—was not as life-threatening as some infants born with Potter's syndrome. Her kidney ultrasound confirmed bilateral polycystic kidneys. Her squished facial features were mild (usually these occur because of compression from insufficient amniotic fluid in utero), and she began to look normal within a few days. Her kidneys' production of urine, which makes up most of the amniotic fluid, had been adequate throughout her mother's pregnancy, so her lungs were only partially underdeveloped. The chest tubes were removed within the first week, and she was easily extubated from the ventilator—taken off it. Her lungs healed completely.

Although Emily continued to produce large volumes of urine during her first few weeks, her kidneys did not function effectively and soon she was in renal failure. My husband was her pediatric nephrologist and we experienced many emotions while working together on Emily's case. It was a challenging and thought-provoking situation. Early on, her parents were, understandably, still reeling from the diagnosis. IPKD causes severe kidney failure and leads to dialysis and ultimately the need for kidney transplantation. Liver scarring is present at birth, but liver dysfunction does not occur until later in childhood. Mortality rates are high. As her parents slowly adjusted to her diagnosis and care needs, within a few weeks Emily was started on peritoneal dialysis, through a catheter entering her abdominal cavity. The dialysis machine cycled fluid into and out of her abdominal cavity to remove chemicals and toxins that built up in the absence of proper kidney function.

Her father, a brilliant chemist and Rice professor, would sit by her side and study the dialysis machine, its settings and functioning. Jeff was a tall, handsome man who was typically quiet, although he seemed to enjoy talking with the pediatric residents and nurses about these settings and how dialysis works. Emily's mother, Patricia, a practicing lawyer, was an attractive, thin woman who looked despondent and seemed always to be on the verge of tears. She expressed breastmilk for her nutritional support and proceeded to cope with having a chronically hospitalized baby, another child at home, and a career. Most days that Patricia came in and out of the unit to see Emily, she looked haggard. Answering her questions and commenting on how cute Emily was always made her smile, though. Unlike a lot of other chronically ill babies, her daughter had a sweet temperament, and I enjoyed pointing this out to her mother. Years later, Patricia recollected that I "was the one who got them thinking of Emily as a person." I didn't have enough free time myself to get to know this mom, or to support her more fully, but my husband did. Emily's parents were agreeable, intelligent, and levelheaded, and I found it painful to watch them handle everything so courageously. Perhaps my husband and I identified with them too much. I often wondered if, in the same situation, I would be as calm as Emily's mother was.

Emily went home on dialysis when she was a few months old. My husband continued to oversee and direct her dialysis and care. In the interim, she required several readmissions to the hospital for various problems, and when she was only two years old, she received a kidney transplant, a gift from her sixty-year-old maternal grandmother. Blood type and various other histocompatibility markers were studied among her family members, and it was determined that Emily and her grandmother were a perfect match. Theirs became a tremendous success story for the hospital renal transplant program. And that wasn't all: Emily was heralded as the first infant to receive dialysis from the time of birth at TCH.

At that time, Anne was a healthy toddler with radiant blue eyes and silky blond hair (just like Emily's). She seemed perfect throughout her infant and toddler years until she began to display intense temper tantrums—rolling on the floor, red-faced, kicking and screaming. I was unprepared for the scorching embarrassment that I felt during Anne's public tantrums. The trials of toddler discipline for both of our children were essential since my husband and I planned to be lenient parents. Our new nanny, Weezie (Louise's nickname), was an energetic, fun-loving caregiver whom I happily employed for three years. She rescued me after the young Rice coed disaster. Weezie was a hefty young African American woman who adored my children. She had the most uplifting attitude and positive outlook. Although Weezie never seemed to worry, I continued to fret about every early childhood issue, including what sort of preschool would best serve my children.

During those early years, I delighted in all the normal things that my children did. David was an active youngster who loved to lay out and play with gigantic Brio train tracks, running them under furniture throughout the living room, adding bridges, switches, and stations. He was also attracted to the piano. By age four he was pecking away at the keys with all the fingers on his left hand and requesting lessons. When Phillip played guitar, he let David strum away while my husband held down the strings on each fret to form chords. Clearly, David enjoyed making music.

Anne thrilled in being carted and pushed around by her brother, especially in large boxes, bins, or hampers. Just looking at Anne always melted my heart. She was so cute with her thick, blond hair, penetrating blue eyes, and naturally red lips. Weezie loved to dress her in pretty outfits with matching hair bows. Once Weezie dressed my children as cowgirl and cowboy, with vests, hats, and boots, and took them to the Houston rodeo livestock show to see the animals. Anne grew to be an opinionated, active, and precious toddler. At age two, she would stare at us, posing defiantly with her hands on her hips, her mischievous expression and blond pigtails bouncing, shaking her head, and saying, "You can't tell me...what to do!" They both loved playing with our wooden, bright red Radio Flyer wagon. Today, my three-year-old granddaughter delights in riding in that same vintage wagon.

Temper tantrums are to be expected in toddlers; however, they can be embarrassing when you're out in public. It's normal for tantrums to emerge between two and three years of age, when children are testing limits. But Anne did the whole routine—lying on the floor, kicking, screaming, and crying. We knew enough to ignore her fits and walk away, but in the drugstore, supermarket, and video store, I got harsh, judgmental looks—the kind that said, "Can't you control your own child?" My husband likes to reminisce about witnessing one of these tantrums in a grocery store aisle. A sweet, older woman walked over to peer at our screaming child. While she looked down at our thrashing toddler, she beckoned everyone nearby to come over and look, too. She gathered three or four other women around Anne, and all of them stood there and gazed down at her. Anne abruptly stopped her tantrum, got up, and walked to her father. I wish we had a video of that moment showing a most effective strategy to quiet an out-of-control child.

During this busy time with two young children and all the issues they presented to me, another memorable patient, baby Catherine, was born in 1990. Her mother was also a bright, busy, young lawyer like Patricia. She caught cytomegalovirus infection from her son. It's a common way for pregnant women to acquire the disease. The toddler gets sick with something like a cold, and the pregnant mother catches a viral infection that is devastating for her fetus. CMV acquired in utero usually leads to overwhelming, ravaging disease. Two intrauterine procedures were performed to remove fetal ascites—fluid in the fetal abdomen—and Catherine was delivered prematurely at 35 weeks and evaluated for congenital CMV.

After Catherine's birth, we examined her blood counts, liver function tests, brain scans, cerebrospinal fluid exam and cultures, retinal exams, and hearing tests. Even though Catherine's symptoms were relatively mild, she had evidence of active infection throughout her body. She had low platelets (blood-clotting cells), hepatitis (liver inflammation), meningitis (spinal fluid infection), and evidence of retinitis (severe eye infection). Unfortunately, she was born with bilateral nerve deafness. If her infection was allowed to proceed untreated, she would be severely affected and end up with significant neurodevelopmental handicaps, mental retardation, and blindness, in addition to her deafness.

Around the time that Catherine was born, a pediatric infectious diseases specialist at TCH and Baylor College of Medicine had just begun a phase two clinical trial of ganciclovir, a drug thought to be effective in the treatment of CMV. Drug dosing still needed to be worked out, and this drug at a higher dose was intended for babies with central nervous system involvement, just like Catherine. This infectious disease doctor was brilliant and had secured a National Institutes of Health grant for this study. NIH grants were a big deal at Baylor and any other academic medical center. Catherine qualified for the trial, and her parents consented eagerly and with great hopefulness. I took care of their daughter during the eight weeks of her ganciclovir therapy.

Because of infection risk, we decided not to insert a central line, so Catherine required many IV insertions over those weeks. In retrospect, inserting a central venous line percutaneously, through the skin, would have prevented her from all those painful IV sticks over the weeks. We checked lab values for drug toxicity, followed her growth and liver function, adjusted feedings, adjusted drug dosing (according to protocol), and updated her parents daily. There were several dreadful IV mishaps (infiltrations) into her forehead and the back of her hand. Twice the drug dosage had to be altered or held because of kidney toxicity or white blood cell abnormalities. As expected, her mother needed a lot of attention and patient explanations throughout this ordeal, but she coped with her infant's illness amazingly well. To me, she always seemed calm and inquisitive. She expressed her breastmilk for her daughter, and since it was culture positive for CMV, we were all worried about possible viral transmission via the breastmilk. Our hope was that the baby would receive more maternal antibodies against CMV than she would receive the virus itself from the breastmilk, but no one knew for certain.

Eight weeks later, after ganciclovir therapy was completed, Catherine was found to be free of the CMV virus. Her treatment was a tremendous success. Because her hearing loss was identified early, and she was fitted with hearing aids around four months of age, she developed language skills normally. From the time of her birth, both she and her family learned to sign. When she was about a year old, Catherine's mother brought her up to the NICU one afternoon after an audiology appointment. She wanted to say hello and was excited to report that her speech development was on target, and that she appeared neurologically normal. Mom took a picture of me holding Catherine.

Two years after I moved to Little Rock, in 1993, her father sent me a copy of the TCH volunteers' magazine, *The Watch*. On the front cover was a darling picture of Catherine at about two years of age. She had sandy curls and was wearing a blue velvet, smocked dress. She was grinning and had a lovely sparkle in her blue eyes. The article recounted her eight weeks of struggles through the ganciclovir trial and highlighted the research of that pediatric infectious disease physician. Since the article made no mention of me, I felt left out and a little jealous. I had done much of the work, but the infectious diseases doctor was the one with the huge grant and the consequential research. Thankfully, Catherine's neurodevelopment remained normal despite her permanent hearing loss. Her thoughtful father wrote me a personal note thanking me for all my efforts, care, and concern. He must have understood how much I genuinely cared about Catherine's well-being and how hard I worked to ensure her recovery. I always felt tremendous gratification when parents recognized my competence and my caregiving.

We maintained contact with Emily's parents after we moved to Arkansas. My husband saw Emily in the summer when she, like the other kidney kids, attended Camp Okawehna in Tennessee each year. The TCH renal dialysis patients always attended camp as a group. It was an overnight camp in the piney woods outside of Nashville. Each June, my husband and the dialysis nurse manager shepherded a large contingency of patients, nurses, dieticians, social workers, and physicians to attend the camp for one week. All the children at Camp O were either on peritoneal or hemodialysis or had already been transplanted. Emily attended camp each summer for several years, from about age eight onward. Like all the other kids there, she played with other children who were just like her and felt normal. These kidney kids, as they were lovingly called, all had lines and tubes sticking out of them, and they all had scars. Most were very short, having had poor growth for many years. But they still loved normal child-like activities—running, playing, kicking, throwing, competing, swimming, making craft items, and performing in talent shows. The final night of Camp O was prom night, for which they all dressed up in formal dresses and suits previously donated and altered by the Junior League of Nashville. The kids danced the night away to songs played by a live band.

Years later, after moving to Austin, we continued to correspond with Emily's parents. We exchanged Christmas cards, family pictures, and personal letters. It was inspiring to watch her parents become champions and activists for organ transplantation. Emily's life was not easy by any estimation. Throughout her childhood, she demonstrated enormous courage in overcoming many complications, infections, and hospitalizations, but Emily never rejected her grandmother's kidney. When she grew to be a teenager, however, her liver function began to fail.

Everyone who knew them viewed Emily's family as strong and loving. From the time Emily was eight years old, her parents lived on campus and served as College Masters at Rice University. As a result, Emily grew up keen on learning, with students all around her. She was a good student herself and was praised by her favorite teacher for "her mind, her wit, and her sense of humor." Despite her chronic illness, Emily loved life and grew to be fiercely independent. She performed in musical theater, played tennis, and hiked in the Colorado Mountains with her family. At home, she played softball, the guitar, and composed songs. Emily continued to do well in school and ultimately attended Trinity University, a small college in San Antonio. She was there for two years before her untimely death at age twenty.

To this day, Emily's mother raises money for Polycystic Kidney Disease research and serves on the board of the International PKD Foundation. When I contacted Emily's father by email, he told me that his daughter's "spirit continued to be very strong in their family." Her big sister is now grown and married with two children of her own, a boy and a girl. They all cherish that Emily's niece is "much like Emily in personality and appearance." This magnanimous man told me how grateful he and his wife were for all our "efforts in saving Emily's life in those first weeks, months, and years."

Recently, I had the good fortune to reconnect with Catherine's mother, who is now living in Austin. I learned that her daughter grew up attending all mainstream schools aided by assistive hearing devices. She and her family used a total communication method called Signed English (in which grammar and syntax are different from American Sign Language). Catherine didn't receive a cochlear implant until she was a teenager. Her neurodevelopment throughout childhood and adolescence remained normal except for deafness and slightly altered speech. Recently, Catherine completed a master's degree in Community and Regional Planning from the University of Texas at Austin. She now works as a hazard mitigation planner for GrantWorks in Austin. She also serves on the board of AURA ATX (An Austin for Everyone). As an advocate for deaf people, she is passionate about bringing disabled perspectives to urban planning.

To their credit, both Catherine and her mother have become advocates for early CMV detection and treatment. Catherine produced a YouTube video and her mother gave presentations around the country highlighting the impact of congenital CMV and the importance of early detection. In fact, Catherine's mother recently lobbied for legislation in Texas that makes CMV educational materials available to the parents of infants, expecting parents, and women who may become pregnant.[1] Educational materials—in both English and Spanish—describe the incidence of CMV, transmission routes, and available preventive measures.

Unfortunately, the additional mandate for targeted screening for CMV didn't pass the Texas legislature. Apparently, the Texas Medical Association was opposed because doctors would have to decide which newborns needed to be treated. I still hope the day will come for universal newborn testing for congenital CMV. And I feel proud of having played a small part contributing to Catherine's health and well-being.

---

1 Texas Senate Bill 791 - Relating to education about congenital cytomegalovirus in infants; passed Sept. 1, 2015.

Chapter 7

HEALING THE HEALERS

My NICU work taught me compassion, empathy, and patience, but I was unprepared for the scorching embarrassment I felt when the preschool teacher sent home a note reporting how my child bit another child. Yes, David never developed temper tantrums, but around three years of age, he began biting, poking, and hitting other children at preschool. As an uninitiated mother, I was clueless about why this behavior occurred there. He had always relished going to school and loved learning new things. The teacher's note didn't explain what happened—it just said that he "bit another child." Reading her note, I felt ashamed. He had long since stopped hurting his sister, so I didn't understand this new behavior. I read that some toddlers around age three struggle with their emotions and resort to biting or hitting to express frustration. At home, we practiced "use your words" and named emotions in most situations. He had heard "biting hurts—we do not bite others" from all of us. Only once did he bite me; in that instance, I abruptly screamed at him (which you're not supposed to do), and he was so startled that he burst into tears. It took lots of hugs and snuggling to calm us both down that day.

Some months later, David's teacher sent home other notes. They told of David poking other children in the face or eyes. Again, I was naive about the cause of this bad behavior. When I met with his teacher, she described him being simply curious and exploring others, and she seemed to take it in stride. He was getting plenty of extra attention at home. But he was getting a lot of timeouts at school. I agonized: How could he think that it was okay to touch or poke other children in the face? It was perplexing since we had not demonstrated any such behavior at home. As I think back on this, I wonder if his toddler aggression reflected boredom. What did it mean that he seemed to be missing social cues while playing with other children? He was a bright child, loved classical music, books, and reading at a young age. Did he need more physical activity? He was sleeping well by then, having no more night terrors. We were puzzled, and I remained continually embarrassed. Thankfully, this aggressive behavior ran its course, too.

I struggled over the decision to keep my children in the church preschool or to enroll them in a private preschool. Fortunately, we attended a Methodist church in which the small preschool was known to be excellent. The preschool teachers there seemed warm, calm, and nonjudgmental. I will never forget when, on "doctor's day," one of David's teachers took me aside after I dropped off some cookies or came in to demonstrate to the children how a stethoscope, otoscope, and tongue blade worked. She said, "you don't need to try so hard" and then she observed that "working mothers volunteer more than stay-at-home mothers." Perhaps that's the case in the early years, but I doubt that it's true overall. She probably told me in hopes that I might relax from my continual efforts to be present for my children. Back then, I do remember many times driving frantically from the hospital to the church. And there was that one afternoon that I forgot to pick up David from preschool. That morning I told Weezie that I would, but I got busy at work and it slipped my mind. After the school called our home phone, Weezie paged me and asked what happened. I was doubly embarrassed— in front of my nanny and the preschool teacher. Fortunately, David was happily playing and unaware when I arrived late that day.

I have a sister-in-law who was the perfect stay-at-home mother. For many years, she was a classic soccer mom—in her case, a baseball mom—for four active children. She was involved in everything her kids did—sports, school, and church. She volunteered often at the schools, she told me, because she could and because she understood that working moms could not. I often wondered if she liked all that volunteering. I tried to enjoy my interactions at my children's schools in the early years, but always found myself feeling rushed or spread too thin.

I began to learn about the Montessori teaching philosophy, and I visited several Montessori schools around Houston. The idea of having my children in a setting that emphasized independence, freedom within limits, and discovery was appealing to me. Although the Montessori schools were quite expensive, they were known for creating a learning environment that assisted in the development of the whole child. Thinking like a pediatrician, it satisfied me that a Montessori school might nurture their cognitive, social, and physical selves, especially since I didn't know how to do that. And so, months later, both David and Anne attended Montessori preschool and kindergarten, and it was all for the best. Both my children seemed to enjoy spending time "teaching" younger children and choosing their own activities.

David came home talking about the "hundred spot." It took me a month to figure out that this was a hundred's board with ten columns and ten rows on which he wrote the numbers from one to one hundred, correctly, at age five. David's favorite activity his first year at St. Stephen's Episcopal Montessori school was "scrubbing tables." This was ironic since he was the messiest child I have ever known. He routinely spilled milk and juice, dropped or smeared food wherever he was eating, left pencil shavings on the floor or carpet after sharpening them, and always wrinkled or ripped every paper worksheet.

When I was a young physician mother trying to acclimate, I realized that I was working too much, frequently fifty to sixty hours a week. When I wasn't in the NICU, I tried to write my first grant application. I remember my work feeling incredibly stressful during that time. It wasn't so much because of the patients themselves; it was everything else—my other efforts to become established in academic medicine. During my second year on faculty, I completed a sophisticated clinical trial of optimal constant positive airway pressure, or CPAP, in the NICU. I asked parents if I could measure their baby's airway pressures, heart rate, and blood pressures, and the pressure in their esophagus, which approximated pleural pressure, the pressure inside their chest. This was done with a plethysmograph, a large stainless steel, multichannel recording device that sat at the bedside while I changed the level of CPAP pressure the baby received through his endotracheal tube. I also tabulated arterial blood oxygen and carbon dioxide levels and blood pH at every level of change in airway pressure.

Twelve sets of brave parents gave consent for this study. It was formidable to do on my own; that was my first mistake. I soon discovered that doing clinical research alone was tense and often frightening. I remember having splitting, pounding headaches when I prepared to study a baby. My senior faculty advisor helped me design the study, analyze the data, and write the paper, but I had been alone obtaining consent and alone standing at the baby's bedside recording measurements. Thank goodness, no baby was harmed by my study—I made sure of that. Ultimately, the paper we wrote about optimal CPAP was published in a prestigious journal.[2] Nevertheless, I chose to discontinue my work with pulmonary function testing. It was too taxing.

Throughout medical school and during my training, I always dreamed of having a career in academic medicine. In that environment, you are expected to serve as a three-legged stool, well-balanced on the legs of patient care, research, and teaching. Academic medicine exists as an interaction between clinical teaching and shared clinical responsibility. The focus is on learning, questioning, and advancing the practice of medicine. In addition to performing research, faculty members teach pediatric residents and medical students, and, in exchange, the residents perform much of the clinical work that keeps the NICU humming. Academic faculty allow residents to learn medicine by practicing on their patients—exactly like an apprenticeship. Residents saw and cared for whatever patients I saw and cared for.

In the beginning I found teaching pediatric residents and medical students enjoyable but demanding. I was grateful to have a superb teaching role model. My mentor, an older, soft-spoken, British-trained professor, Dr. Jack Rudolph, started the neonatology division at Baylor. Dr. Rudolph was short and rotund,

---

2   Optimal Constant Positive Airway Pressure in Hyaline Membrane Disease. by S Landers, TN Hansen, AJS Corbet. *Pediatr Res.* 1986; 20: 884-889.

with a receding gray hairline that highlighted his forehead and full cheeks. He wore gold spectacles and liked to grin, producing dimples in his pudgy cheeks. Dr. Rudolph was gifted in teaching students and residents. We all called him "the Boss," and his weekly presentations were called "Rudolph rounds." No one missed Rudolph rounds. He showed slides of interesting findings, birth defects, and the like. His slide collection was famous and included photographs of virtually every disease, disorder, and condition affecting the newborn. These photographs were later compiled into an encyclopedic *Atlas of the Newborn*, which was published in five volumes.

In addition to his vast collection of photographs, Dr. Rudolph taught us the Socratic method of teaching. He would show a slide and, in his distinctive British accent, ask, "Oh, what do you see?" or "What do you think this could be?" When we were uncertain of some skin condition, we would escort him into the nursery to see the baby. While everyone gathered around, he would carefully and slowly pick up and examine the baby and say, "Don't touch baby. Tell me what you notice." His gentle nature was not the least bit intimidating. Medical students and residents delighted in his presentations, listening to him, and answering his questions, often wrongly, without feeling threatened or embarrassed.

In the NICU, I learned to teach using the Socratic method that Dr. Rudolph modeled so well. I would often interrupt residents, or NNPs, and ask what they saw, or what they thought was the differential diagnosis. I asked them what they were thinking about and what were the treatment options. This was a cooperative but slightly argumentative dialogue with them. It was based on asking and answering questions to stimulate critical thinking and to draw out ideas. Over the years, most pediatric residents and NNPs seemed to like it.

However, pediatric residents in general tended not to appreciate their NICU rotations. Many felt abused by the amount of scut work that was required. Ordinarily they wrote daily orders, including hyperalimentation fluids, checked lab results, gathered X-rays, and adjusted ventilator settings. They attended high-risk deliveries and were required to learn proper resuscitation of newborns. Some residents relished performing procedures, inserting umbilical arterial and venous catheters, chest tubes, and endotracheal tubes. Teaching these procedures, however, was extremely time-consuming and required great patience. Because they were techniques that most pediatricians didn't need to know for a general office practice, some of them resisted the experience.

During my early attending years, I continued to recognize and deal with my own anger issues. Sometimes I slipped and scolded a pediatric resident for doing something stupid the night before, usually the result of their not calling for help. For one year, I worked with one research nurse who chatted incessantly and made me furious, but I never reproached her. She was a nice, older NICU nurse whom Dr. Rudolph had highly recommended to me. So, instead, I fumed internally and developed throbbing headaches whenever she was around "helping me."

Most of my angry outbursts occurred at home, directed at poor David when he acted out. Fortunately, my headaches resolved, and as I continued in cognitive behavioral therapy, I learned to be a more patient mother and set consistent limits. Commonly, I gave myself time-outs, during which I would leave my child's presence, find some quiet place to sit for a few minutes, and calm down. Although time out did not seem to influence David, the technique worked wonders for me.

Away from work, I used to enjoy quick escapes into the nearby neighborhoods. After Phillip was home and fixing dinner, I dressed for a run and struck out for the Rice University area a few blocks from us. I took the bridge over Highway 59 and ran into the upper-crust Southampton residential area. Running a few miles up and down the lengths of North and South Boulevards, admiring the elegant, old stately homes—some were mansions, shaded by huge oak trees—was both relief and refresher. I wasn't a fast runner, so the time was as much for exercise as it was for thought and reflection. Phillip and I tried several different workout classes together, such as yoga-aerobics and beginning mat Pilates, but they didn't stick. Regular exercise takes commitment and is rarely compatible with raising small children.

While we were living and practicing in Houston, my husband and I had the great fortune of participating in a group called Healing the Healers. A Baylor psychiatrist, who was also a Methodist minister, created and facilitated our group. There were six couples who met every other Sunday evening for nearly three years. There were four physician couples and two psychologist couples. Initially, we met at the church, and later in each other's living rooms, more comfortably seated, munching on snacks. Our facilitator prompted us with questions.

He subscribed to the notion that most people become doctors to care for others because they were somehow lacking in that care for themselves. An alternative theory held that the helping of others is a means of pushing our own needs and anxieties into the background. The psychologist Carl Jung called this person the "wounded healer" and wrote that "it is his own hurt that gives a measure of his power to heal." These theories all suggested that we needed to deal with not only our current feelings, but also our old wounds, so that we could function as better caregivers.

Our Healing the Healers group discussed everything from marriage relationships to parenting our children, and even dealing with our own parents. We talked about our feelings, and we spoke less often about our patients and problems at work. Our group's goals were to provide mutual support and to improve our understanding of the stresses of being caregivers. Our skilled psychiatrist facilitator showed each of us ways in which we allowed our jobs to overtake our lives and marriages.

This wonderful psychiatrist taught me that I was comparable to a bottomless cup, full of caring, compassion, skills, and responsibility, pouring out parts of myself for my patients and my work. I figured out quickly that empty cups do not serve well. He helped me recognize that I was not yet in the habit of actively refilling my cup, and he taught me to identify and create effective ways to do that. For instance, my friend Patty, a clinical psychologist specializing in infertility, bought herself a bouquet of fresh flowers every Friday. Inspired by her, I got myself a bouquet at least once a month. I tried to go running twice a week, and I made a point of attending St. Paul's Methodist church services and my adult Sunday school class. St. Paul's had a magnificent pipe organ in the sanctuary that produced heavenly music every Sunday—Bach, Beethoven, and others. The organist often played an additional song after the service was over, so those of us who liked the music could linger and enjoy it for ourselves.

I soon discovered, however, that teaching children's Sunday school was not for me. After attempting it one spring, I gave up since I was unable to engage the rowdy children without getting angry at them, which defeated the whole purpose. When I found some free time, I created several colorful counted cross-stitch nursery or crewel decorations for my children. There were other samplers that I gave as gifts or wedding presents to friends. Sitting still and stitching in the evening, or while children were napping, was always relaxing and oftentimes felt meditative.

There was another important thing that the brilliant psychiatrist taught me. By the time we joined the support group, my husband and I had established a parenting pattern in which I acted as the "bad cop," and he assumed the role of "good cop." Our leader helped me realize that if I was acting as the bad cop, as it were, then I should be able to ask for assistance when needed, from my "deputy." He taught me the wisdom of "deputizing my husband" when it was necessary. I taught myself to pause and say, "I need a deputy," and be specific about what we both needed to do. Slowly, I learned to ask for the help I needed, and to be unambiguous with those requests. Now I understand why many female physicians are, like me, typically hyper-responsible and attempt to control everything for their children and families—and much later recognize their own exhaustion or burnout.

Once I arranged a six-year-old birthday party for David and hired a magician. We invited his entire class, and all the children showed up. The magician wowed eighteen first graders on our back deck for over one hour. Fortunately, I gave my husband a detailed list of all his jobs before and during the party, and he did them. As a result, I didn't feel stressed or crazy that day, but joyful, and David's party was a huge success.

The psychiatrist pressed us all to examine our relationships with our parents as we struggled to raise our own children. He encouraged journaling and suggested that we write letters to our parents, expressing our feelings, even if we never mailed them. I wrote a long letter to my father once, admonishing him for all his rage attacks and physical harm to me and my siblings during my childhood. It was freeing to write that indignant letter to him. At that time, I had yet to forgive him for his bad behaviors when I was a little girl. By then, I realized that his example taught me most of my own abnormal behaviors. Our collective group willingly discussed these sorts of important issues, and the insights we developed in that couples' support group over a three-year period were golden. I still miss that wonderful group of big-hearted healers.

Both of my children appeared to be happy and thriving in the Montessori school. I was improving in my efforts to deputize my husband, and I was learning ways to fill up my cup. I became less stressed and recognized fewer angry-mommy moments. Then, about five years into our marriage and busy, working lives, I talked my husband into having a third child. We were both from large families, and at that time, I believed that two children were not enough. Conceiving my last pregnancy took some time and effort, however, and Laura came along when I was nearly forty years old. Having a third child ended up feeling like admitting critically ill triplets to the NICU at 2 a.m. No one warned me how tired I would feel as a forty-year-old working mother with three children.

Chapter 8

TRIAL IN A NEW NICU

My first eight years as an attending neonatologist in Houston flew by. Working in the NICU full-time was invigorating, and mostly enjoyable. Moreover, I was fortunate that my department allowed me three maternity leaves of eight weeks each. The neonatology division at Baylor was huge, employing over fifteen faculty and nine fellows. Attending faculty taught residents and fellows in two NICUs—one at TCH and one at Jefferson Davis Hospital. Each fellow conducted clinical or laboratory research under a faculty member's direct supervision. The neo program there was highly structured and followed a formal teaching curriculum for pediatric residents and neo fellows. Medical students rotated through our vast intermediate care and newborn nurseries and were provided ample time to examine normal newborns and well premature infants.

My clinical schedule, when I was "on-service" in the NICU, was livable. Attending neonatologists worked ten-hour weekdays for one week, rounded for several hours on weekend days, worked ten-hour days during the next week, followed by a weekend off. We took some night call, but the fellows took the bulk of it. Two attendings worked together in the larger TCH NICU, each supervising the care of around fifteen patients, which made it easy to collaborate and discuss problematic or complex patients. Teaching conferences were held each weekday at noon for residents and fellows. Faculty and fellows took turns giving presentations, some formal, and others informal white-board talks.

This large group of neonatologists and fellows maintained mostly pleasant interactions. There were very few personality conflicts. As the clinical service grew rapidly during the 1980s, several other fellows and I were hired to join the faculty after completing our fellowship training. As a result, we all knew each other well and enjoyed shared social events and "journal club" gatherings monthly at one another's homes for literature review and discussion. At a farewell party given in my honor, I was told by Charleta Guillory, an African-American colleague, that she would miss me because she considered me to be the "conscience of the group." By then, I was known for voicing my opinions, and, in contrast, Charleta was known for being a quiet, caring, and cooperative neonatologist. She was lovely to work with, and I considered her remark a sideways compliment. I did not fully appreciate this academic environment—the one in which I was trained and later worked as an attending—until I left it.

Then, in 1991, everything changed. My husband was offered a new job as pediatric nephrology division chief and a promotion to full professor at the medical school in Little Rock, Arkansas. At that time in our marriage, his career seemed more important than mine, a sticky issue for lots of working moms. We agreed this was a great move for him since I was busy being a mom of three and working full-time. My new job in Arkansas would be one of the regular neonatology attending staff. However, it was disappointing that no promotion was offered to me. We were both to be employed by the University of Arkansas for Medical Sciences (UAMS). David was seven and Anne was four years old at the time. My third child, Laura, was born in February before we moved in June. I was unprepared for the changes and upheaval that were to come.

Our move to Arkansas created a mountain of new tasks for me as a mother— finding a new home, a new school, and a new nanny. Luckily, we located a perfect, and larger, house with a big backyard, but I needed to secure a nanny and decide on new schools for the kids. The public elementary school in our Little Rock neighborhood was large, average, and uninviting. There were several private schools to choose from and I visited them all. A small private school in a nearby neighborhood was known for having great teachers. Even though my husband and I both were products of public education, and we believed in that, for the time being we chose the little Anthony School closer into town.

Then I set out to find the right nanny. That took more effort, but she also worked out soon enough. I used a service to narrow down my choices and obtain background checks. I personally called each and every reference the women gave me. After conducting six candidate interviews, I decided on the young wife of a pharmacy student. She had years of babysitting experience and was eager to earn money for their living expenses while her husband was in school. Tammy had a sweet personality and terrific energy.

I began work just as the children's school year got underway and immediately found my new neonatology job to be a hot mess. My boss was an Arkansas "good old boy," born and raised in the area. Older than I was, he was trained locally, never venturing out to a larger, academic medical center. He was extremely old-fashioned and believed that doctors should make rounds daily for a month at a time. So, like the other doctors in my new group, I did just that. I kissed my kids goodbye and trudged in to care for sick and premature infants every day—thirty days in a row—for many months of those first few years. It felt like being on submarine duty.

At work I was confronted with a lousy secretary. The higher NICU patient load and the burden of a horrendous call schedule were brutal. Before our move, I did not understand this would be my fate, and I labored through many ten-hour days in the NICU and took night call in the hospital twice each week. There were "night-rider" doctors, both a resident and neonatologist, who covered the units at night. However, the daytime NICU work was relentless. In contrast, my husband took call from home and went into the hospital for rounds every third weekend, so he was at home to care for our children on the weekends when I worked.

UAMS had NICUs in two different hospitals that were covered by only seven neonatologists. We did have a few months off—to write papers, read journals, and prepare lectures. But the months that we were "on service" were killers. For the first few years I worked seven or eight out of every twelve months "on-service." Unbelievably, one neonatologist routinely made teaching rounds with pediatric residents on twenty-five to thirty babies each day in the Arkansas Children's Hospital (ACH) NICU. You started in the morning after report was given, rounded all day long, examining and discussing each baby, and finished up in the late afternoon. A few procedures were thrown into the mix of this routine, plus the occasional ECMO (extracorporeal membrane oxygenation) baby that demanded your presence in a separate smaller unit.

This kind of NICU care—in which residents did the bulk of the work without fellows around—really strained my personal style and habit of attempting to know everything about each patient, much less visiting with their parents or calling referring doctors. My first year there, my teaching rounds shortened, and I was forced to rely on the residents more than I was accustomed. But, this kind of attending coverage always felt dangerously inadequate to me, and I feared overlooking some resident's mistake. The University Hospital NICU was smaller, with only eighteen beds, and provided us more time to think and teach.

A truly unforgettable moment occurred shortly after our move. Anne was four and a half years old, sick with fever, an ear infection, and she was tucked into her bed that morning. After talking with Tammy, our nanny, and giving her instructions for acetaminophen and the antibiotic, I plodded upstairs to say goodbye to Anne. After explaining that I had to go to work and that Tammy would take care of her today, she asked me why I had to leave. I answered that I had to go into the hospital and take care of sick babies. She looked at me point-blank, frowned, and said, "But I'm a sick baby, too." I paused, pulled the imaginary knife out of my chest, hugged, and kissed her, told her that I loved her, and went in to work. It was that tough to be working full-time in my new environment. I felt horrible, and guilty, and angry that day. These feelings erupted often throughout those first few years in Arkansas, but I continued to work full-time.

Breastfeeding my third child went flawlessly for one year, despite the prolonged eight-month period of pumping breastmilk once back at work. Snide comments about my efforts to pump breastmilk at work were irritating and the NICU provided little privacy for pumping, but I desperately wanted to continue nursing my youngest, and last child, for as long as possible. It was reassuring to me that Laura was an easy baby and toddler throughout all the turmoil brought on by my new job.

During my months off-service, I attempted to complete editions on a paper that had been provisionally accepted for publication. I also initiated a new clinical research project and wrote a grant for our center to become a member of the NICHD Neonatal Network. By doing this, I strived to prove myself as an academic neonatologist, since our center had a great mix of both inborn and outborn babies (for comparisons). In so doing, I worked with a statistician in the pediatrics department who helped me immensely, and we succeeded in writing several papers together. When not on-service—freed from teaching procedures to pediatric residents and talking to parents—I supervised the development of a new mothers' milk bank at the children's hospital.

Unfortunately, the clinical patient care NICU schedule improved minimally throughout my first three years there. I will never forget one conversation with my boss, describing to him how troublesome it was to find a nanny who would work more than fifty hours a week. He smiled at me and said calmly, "Well then, you need a weekend nanny, too." I never did figure out if he was kidding, or just heartless.

My division chief, and my boss, was named John Bennings, but everyone called him "Doc B." All the nurses and residents loved him; he was clearly the king of his territory. He enjoyed bedside teaching but employed no structured curriculum. Over the years, he had personally built the NICU and the neonatal transport service at ACH. I often heard "Doc B. did this" and "Doc B. said that." Whatever he said, went, regardless of recent literature to the contrary. Our division meetings were unstructured and haphazard. In his defense, during my first year there, he allowed me to initiate a program to follow NICU clinical outcomes so that we could assess our clinical practices. (Of course, this process was routine at TCH.) But he and I never really got along well. He must have perceived that I was frustrated and unhappy, however he never attempted to address my concerns.

I did not hate everything about practicing neonatology in Little Rock. There was a plethora of interesting and complex patients and some high-quality programs. ACH had a phenomenal transport helicopter service that brought sick infants and children into ACH from all around the state. There was an excellent extracorporeal membrane oxygenation (ECMO) program run by this tall, handsome cardiovascular surgeon. He was not only brilliant, but also wacky and acted out his real cowboy—try anything—mentality. Neonatal ECMO had been well established by 1991, and so he and his team experimented with pediatric (big kids) and mobile ECMO.

Learning how to effectively manage ECMO patients was a relief to me since TCH did not have an ECMO program in the NICU when I departed. In Arkansas, meconium aspiration syndrome was the most common diagnosis qualifying a baby for ECMO, probably because babies were born out in the hinterlands without a pediatrician in attendance or nearby to suction meconium and properly care for the baby. When these babies got sick after a stressful birth, they were flown into the ACH NICU. When our conventional NICU therapy failed—defined as a greater than a fifty percent chance of dying—they qualified for ECMO. We always had one or two babies on ECMO at once.

Fortunately, I gained some points with the NICU nursing staff by creating a mother's own Milk Bank at ACH. Surprisingly, it was not difficult to convince my division chief to hire a lactation consultant (LC) strictly to serve our NICU mothers and babies. Doc B. was a big breastfeeding proponent, and he bought into the notion that her salary would be covered by income from Milk Bank charges. (I set up the new Milk Bank at ACH like the one we all appreciated at TCH.) Our new milk bank was profitable within one year, and we doubled the number of mothers willing and able to express breast milk for their sick and preterm babies. The second year we doubled NICU breastfeeding rates again. And the nurses approved of my choice of LC.

Sandy was a NICU-RN in her late forties, also a bright and experienced LC. She had a sweet smile, a genuine chuckle, and was warm and soft-spoken. The mothers all liked her, too. In addition, the nurses appreciated not having to deal with this aspect of neonatal care. They were busy with other things and often had little time to help a mom breastfeed her baby. A few of the NICU nurses thought breastfeeding was nasty or dirty, a prejudice still held throughout the South at that time. Sandy convinced them otherwise. As Sandy worked her magic, the NICU nurses came to appreciate those tender moments when moms would attempt to breastfeed their premature infants. One of my great regrets is neglecting to write up our ACH NICU milk bank experience for publication. I failed to make the time to write that paper, but I loved working with Sandy and directing the Milk Bank program. Back then in the early 1990s, having a designated LC and a mother's own milk bank contained within the NICU was still a new idea and describing the structure and function of ours could have provided a format for others.

One unforgettable patient at ACH was a small baby boy who was flown in by Life Flight for surgery. The pediatric surgeon repaired his tracheoesophageal fistula and esophageal atresia shortly after his arrival the night before. Few questions were asked. These are serious birth defects involving the airway and food tube, in which there is a fistula (connection) between the trachea (airway) and the esophagus (food tube). In addition, the esophagus ends in a blind pouch (atresia). The next morning, after examining this baby on rounds I noted that he had many physical characteristics of Trisomy 18— microcephaly (a small head), cleft palate, abnormal hands and feet, and a heart murmur indicating a significant heart defect. The genetics specialist agreed with me and the DNA blood test confirmed the diagnosis within two days. Mortality rates then for babies with Trisomy 18 were ninety-five to one hundred percent, with very few surviving until twelve months of age (only those without heart disease).

Unfortunately, this baby's heart defect precluded his survival, so I counseled his parents that we should take the baby off the ventilator, and if he lived a while, take him home to die. They were keen on that idea and hoped that he would live long enough to meet his big sister at home. The pediatric surgeon was furious at our decision, furious at me, screaming, red-faced, in-the-middle-of-the-NICU mad. I could not tell whether he had another reason besides the baby's death adversely affecting his surgical statistics. He obviously felt that he owned this patient. (He certainly acted like he owned other surgical babies in the NICU and wanted his fellows to manage them, regardless of whether they knew how. He was unaware that we followed his residents and fellows around to ensure orders were correct.) I was embarrassed by his outburst but remained quiet and steadfast. From my point of view, he should never have done the surgical procedure until we understood fully his diagnosis and the extent of his birth defects. From his point of view, I should have included him in the discussion, and as a result, we never got along after our conflict over that case.

When you relocate to another medical center, you quickly observe practices and procedures that are different. I asked lots of questions and did not have the prudence to keep my opinions to myself. I believe now that my questioning their practices was interpreted as criticism. Nevertheless, there was one condition that I could not leave alone. I noticed a high prevalence of severe retinopathy of prematurity (ROP), one of the gravest complications of prematurity. We experienced many fewer cases of severe ROP at TCH despite having several clinical trials ongoing to study ROP there. An excellent pediatric ophthalmologist at Baylor, Dr. Helen Hittner, was famous for her vitamin E studies and early ROP treatment. She was one of an international group of experts who created appropriate nomenclature for the disease. She taught us all so much about this major complication of prematurity. Moreover, at TCH we employed oxygen use protocols that allowed nurses and respiratory therapists to adjust oxygen levels without specific doctor's orders. Data published around that time suggested that high oxygen levels exacerbated ROP. At ACH, the residents and nurses allowed arterial blood oxygen levels to remain high for long periods of time waiting on orders to change the levels.

Ventilated babies receiving oxygen for various lung diseases are exposed to varying oxygen levels and the amount delivered is changed throughout the day, in response to the baby's needs. Higher oxygen levels are necessary when babies are sickest, and oxygen levels are weaned (turned down slowly) during the recovery phase. Blood gases are checked frequently during the acute phase of illness. However, a nurse or respiratory therapist might turn up the oxygen on the ventilator and easily overshoot the desired blood oxygen range. This tactic was routine in the ACH NICU before suctioning and when a baby turned blue from crying. Then the new, higher oxygen level would remain elevated for some time. I was astonished when I heard my boss jokingly refer to this slow turn-down approach as "weaning oxygen at a blinding pace." My focus on ROP and our management of oxygen levels undoubtedly irritated some of the NICU nurses and a few of my colleagues.

All babies develop and mature their retinae in a low oxygen environment, the uterus. Babies make mostly fetal hemoglobin, which binds tightly to oxygen. When babies are born prematurely, they are placed in a relatively higher oxygen environment, and given adult blood transfusions, consisting mostly of hemoglobin A, which releases oxygen easily. When we treat their lung disease with oxygen and mechanical ventilation, they are temporarily exposed to higher oxygen levels. Extremely preterm babies need low arterial oxygen levels, and levels that are stable, not rising and falling. No peaks and no valleys while their retinae are developing.

With the help of a pediatric resident interested in ophthalmology, I conducted a retrospective study of blood arterial oxygen levels and ROP. We reviewed our babies' blood gas data for two years and found an alarming amount of hyperoxia, excessive arterial oxygen levels. We also found an alarming amount of severe ROP, the kind that leads to retinal detachment (blindness) and requires surgery to prevent or treat this complication. By happenstance, a PhD researcher in ophthalmology had moved to Little Rock the year before and was conducting research in his laboratory with a rat model for ROP. Dr. John Penn studied how oxygen exposure stimulated new blood vessel development in the animal retinas, called angiogenesis, a major component of ROP. It was inspiring to talk with him about his rat data and seek his help in assessing our data. His excitement about our clinical study encouraged me to analyze the data and publish our findings, and that felt reassuring.

We analyzed data for hundreds of arterial blood gas levels—absolute numbers and the degree of change up and down—and correlated them to the degree of ROP that each baby developed. Doc B. allowed me to spearhead a quality improvement (QI) team and we developed a new, strict oxygen use protocol for the ACH NICU. The doctors, nurses, and respiratory therapists all cooperated after extensive educational briefings, and, as a result, the rates of severe ROP began to decrease over the next six months. A few years later, Dr. Penn played a major role in ensuring that these data—describing how hyperoxia and oxygen variability contributing to severe ROP—were published.[3] Others around the

---

3   Arterial oxygen fluctuation and retinopathy of prematurity in very-low-birth-weight infants. York JR, Landers S, Kirby RS, Arbogast PG, Penn JS. *J Perinatol.* 2004 Feb; 24(2):82-7.

country were recognizing similar findings, and I felt gratified to have brought an important and worthwhile change to my new NICU.

In 1993, after being on faculty at UAMS for two years, I was finally promoted to associate professor with tenure. I greatly resented not being promoted during my first year there. Once my promotion came through it did not feel like much of an accomplishment. In fact, I perceived the delay in my academic promotion as a traumatic insult. My personal work ethic, typical hyper-responsibility, and tendency toward perfectionism, set me up for continuing disappointments in my new job. Looking back now, I must have made up my mind to hate it there. Everything felt like a fight, or a struggle, and I never felt appreciated in that environment.

That said, there were some enjoyable times spent with our Women in Academic Medicine faculty group. One experience there did feel satisfying. My fondest memory of academic life at UAMS was our women physicians' group. The dean of the medical school recognized that women faculty did not get promoted as quickly as the men did. This was true in many other medical schools, in fact. Several provocative papers describing this issue were published around that time. Our dean allowed us to bring in speakers to discuss academic advancement for the women faculty. Our women's group had regular meetings in which experienced women faculty, those who were full professors, gave advice to us younger ones.

The best "Women in Medicine" seminar that I ever attended was given by Pat Heim, PhD, who wrote and published the book *Hardball for Women*.[4] She described to us how men and women work differently—whether in business or in medicine—emphasizing how women were raised culturally dissimilar from men. From a young age, girls try to get along and learn to play together. We care about each other's feelings and we do not like working, or playing, with anyone we do not like. Growing up as boys, men learn to play for a team, or for a coach, whether they like him or not. They don't care as much about feelings. This is a vast oversimplification, but you get the point. Dr. Heim helped us discover how we practiced medicine, and pursued promotion, differently from

---

4   *Hardball for Women: Winning at the Game of Business.* Third edition. by Pat Heim, Tammy Hughes, and Susan K. Golant

men. Throughout all my years in practice I still believe that she is correct about gender differences in how women work.

While negotiating all these challenges at work, my older daughter began to tell me about her fears of robbers and burglars. At four years of age, she started biting her nails and wetting the bed. My son was having a tough school transition, from Montessori to traditional, and displaying socially immature and disruptive behaviors. I was too overwhelmed to recognize that what each child needed during that time was me—more mommy time—and my reassurance. I was just trying to stay afloat professionally, and I failed to realize how to help my children. Clearly, my sense of balance between medicine and motherhood was unstable.

Chapter 9

MATERNAL DETERIORATION

I n my new Little Rock practice group, there were two male neonatologists whom I often joined for lunch in the hospital cafeteria. They both had small children and understood that attending school events was important to me. One of them had a child in the same school and he graciously agreed to cover me when I needed to leave work and rush to the school for an event or a meeting. We often talked about our attempts to be there for our children, and both heard me complain about our call schedule (compared with the less rigorous one I had in Houston). They disliked the overwhelming hours of NICU work while on-service at ACH, too, and both heard my complaints as validation that we needed more faculty members (i.e. less call) in our division. I was the catalyst for their efforts to convince Doc B. that we should hire additional faculty.

My situation was a tremendous personal challenge: We left Houston where I trained and worked for ten years, where I was married and had all my babies. There I had a network of friends who trained together, got married and delivered babies around the same time. I left behind the love and care of my friends and my church community. Our move turned out to be a monumental adjustment for me. The memory of crying on the phone with my Houston pastor as we prayed together is still vivid in my mind. During our first year in Little Rock, with little social support, I became a resentful, unhappy wife, and a tense, exhausted mother. In addition to my spending too many nights on-call in the hospital away from my family, I found myself not using my scarce time off to replenish myself. I began to carry my stress and worries home from work, and often yelled at my children. Laura was still a baby when I turned forty amid that first chaotic year. Forty is a difficult birthday for many women, even without a new baby, a major move, and a new job.

Many of us feel doubts about our ability to be a good mother, especially with anxiety from changes in work and home routines after having a baby, and like me, many of us have an unrealistic need to be a perfect mom. I had always been a high energy person, but now I felt burdened by all these stressors, and I began to slowly fall apart—I became clinically depressed. In my mind, life was horrible, and everything became a chore. I found myself in one continual dark mood. I did not eat much, and I could not sleep. When I did sleep, I awoke early at 4 a.m. or 5 a.m. When I awoke early my mind buzzed with papers, and promotion, and meetings, and call schedules. It was an incessant jumble of thinking that never went anywhere.

I finally realized this was depression when one day in the NICU I found myself standing at a baby's bedside, talking with the residents, unable to make a simple therapeutic decision: should we try indomethacin, a drug that constricted the PDA (patent ductus arteriosus), or should we proceed straight to surgical ligation? After describing my bewildering and gloomy feelings to a colleague at work, a critical care physician, she recommended a good psychiatrist. He put me on an antidepressant right away. Thankfully, the medicine worked, and along with his weekly cognitive behavioral therapy sessions, my depression began to slowly lift.

While I attempted to assimilate and contribute during those first years in Little Rock, my psychiatrist helped me to set priorities and goals for my life, my children, and my work. He facilitated my sorting through problems with marriage, career, clinical research, childcare, and work-life balance. That sorting required tremendous emotional effort, and my ongoing work in the NICU with critically ill babies seemed far easier. My life as a mother did not stop during this time, and I dealt with Anne's fears and bedwetting, and David's poking other children at school.

My husband was having a terrific time, getting lots done as division chief, and with plenty of help—"hot and cold running nurses" and a devoted, excellent secretary to attend to his needs and schedule. In contrast, I described my life to my therapist as the man on The Ed Sullivan Show who spun plates. You may have seen him on TV starting a plate to spinning on the end of a thin stick. He would run around the stage spinning the sticks between his hands to keep them moving, adding one stick and plate spinning, then more sticks and plates, one after another. He ran around frenetically intercepting any wobbling plates and spinning their sticks again, to keep all the plates spinning so none would fall. When I described this analogy to my psychiatrist, he chuckled out loud. But then he smiled and said, "Take down some of the plates."

It was astonishing to me that he could see a solution. From then on, I began to examine my plates, and decided which ones to take down, and which ones to let wobble. During that process, over the subsequent two years, I began to improve. In retrospect, it is surprising that I could work full-time during an episode of major depression. I suspect that most people struggling with a major depressive episode need to shift gears into part-time work or take time off as a short-term medical leave.

My psychiatrist and I discussed each and every plate, all my issues. It was vital for me to choose which ones to let go, because I had always done too much. Choosing to do any less with my children than I already did was not an option. However, I could leave work earlier on the days I was not on-service. I could decline another research project and concentrate on finishing those in progress. I would not stop teaching. I loved teaching, but I could refrain from volunteering to prepare formal presentations, unless it was my turn. I could worry less about new publications and simply finish the old ones. Hardest to deal with was the spinning plate that represented my husband and my resentment of his easy life. I could not stand that his life seemed effortless and that he was contented with his job. Within two years, he became vice-chairman of the department for education, a marvelous new position, so my resentment plate continued to wobble on.

Despite there being two women in my new NICU physician group, they were both unfriendly. One was quite stiff and sour and never spoke much to anybody, and the other was bossy, outgoing, and gregarious. I asked her questions about how things were done there and why. She always answered me nicely but kept saying that "we should have lunch and talk." We never did. Like our boss, she was an Arkansas native, and her kids were grown. She gave me the distinct feeling that she did not appreciate what I had to offer their practice. In retrospect, it is clear to me now that one should not ask questions when one is thrown into a new practice, at least not for the first year or so. My questions were undoubtedly interpreted as implied criticisms.

It is surprising, and a little sad, that these two women neonatologists made no attempts to befriend me. Besides my two welcoming male colleagues, I found only one good friend in Little Rock. Out of the blue, one afternoon my new best friend, Becky, holding her infant daughter, found me reading in my tiny office. Becky was a slender, young brunette, internist-turned-pathology resident. Like me, she was adjusting to a new baby, a new town, and career. She and her husband had just moved from North Carolina, and they shared mutual friends with whom we trained years before in Houston. Those friends instructed her to find us since her husband had just joined our pediatric department at UAMS. We saw Becky and Gary often over those six years in Little Rock, enjoying lunch together on the weekends, or sharing dinner with all our children on Friday nights.

Gary and their daughters attended one church and I took my kids to another church on Sundays I was off. Becky and my husband waited in a coffee shop and chatted until we all assembled after church for Sunday dinner. Becky and my husband got along well since they shared a distinctive sarcasm, disrespect for organized religion, and tremendous intelligence. Like me, Becky had some adjustments to make to a new baby and another residency. Unlike me, Becky valued living in Little Rock, even though she had to drive thirty miles every day to her pathology practice in a smaller town. She liked the slower pace, the better public schools on their side of town, her long walks, her dogs, her birdwatching, and the extra time she had for reading. Me, not so much.

There were plenty of complex and difficult patients in my new NICU, but one case there was truly unforgettable. My most memorable Arkansas moment transpired during a family conference before discharging a preterm baby whom I had cared for in the NICU for six months. A frail teenage mother had delivered her son months before and her baby was transported from a small-town hospital deep in the Ozark Mountains to ACH. This little guy had a complicated course, but his young mother was dutifully by his bedside as often as she could be. She lived nearby at the Ronald McDonald House for families. Her son slowly overcame all his medical problems and was feeding well enough to go home on oxygen by nasal cannula (a tube that sits right at the nostrils). He needed a home monitor, in case of continued apnea, breathing pauses that were life-threatening. This young mother had learned how to take care of him in every way. She even learned how to perform CPR, or cardiopulmonary resuscitation.

Her family was very poor, so our social worker needed to have their home checked for electricity, running water, and a phone line. Local officials gave her the green light. The family who arrived for our discharge conference included the teen mom and both of her parents. The social worker, discharge case manager, and I were in attendance and reviewed his course and ongoing care needs. I asked about the baby's father and whether he was in the picture, because I wanted to know if he needed CPR training, too. The young mother initially said nothing, but then looked down at her hands folded in her lap and said quietly that her brother was the father. I gasped, hopefully quietly. Then the baby's grandfather gruffly said, "Yeah, we've had lots of trouble with that boy. He knocked up his other sister last year." I sat upright, literally felt nauseous, and wished I could scream at that man. I did not, but after exchanging nervous looks with the social worker, I faked a page on my beeper, excused myself and left the room. I had never been so close to a culture of incest, poverty, and a poor family's struggle to survive. It was a startling and unsettling revelation, but I should not have left the room that day. I should have sat there quietly and listened.

After Tammy's husband graduated and they moved away, I hired our next nanny. Betty was an unforgettable, sixty-year-old, petite woman from North Little Rock. She had a lively personality, a sweet smile, and cheerful disposition.

She came to us with incredibly good references. Betty wore lots of makeup, had permed hair, and was always dressed nicely. I liked her distinctive, twangy, Southern accent. Betty turned out to be a wonderful nanny, always happy, and great with the kids. She cleaned, did laundry, drove, and met me places with the children. She supervised schoolwork and kept track of play dates. She came to soccer games and swim practice. She worked for us for over two years, until one day when my neighbor called to inform me that Betty had a heart attack. Apparently, Betty tried to call 911 and collapsed, leaving Laura to speak into the phone to tell the dispatcher, "Betty's sick." My neighbor cared for Laura while the paramedics bundled up Betty for a ride to the hospital. After collecting Anne and David from school, we frantically drove home. I wondered about what happened, tried to explain what I knew to the kids, worried about how unstable Betty might be, and what I would do about childcare. It was frightening.

The next day I proceeded to visit Betty in the University Hospital, where she was admitted. She was on cardiac telemetry, continuous heart monitoring, and seemed glum sitting up in her hospital bed. I asked about the heart attack, asked if she was in pain, and if she was getting her questions answered. Then, I asked how I could help. She seemed so quiet and sad, but just smiled weakly and said, "No, I'll be fine." She did not sound like herself. Assuming that she felt badly, I left her room and proceeded to the nursing station to find her cardiologist. No one was around, so I peeked inside her hospital chart. Her admitting diagnosis was "60 y. o. Caucasian female w/ cocaine overdose + cardiac arrhythmia."

I was absolutely stunned. At that time, I was forty-four years old, and having practiced medicine for many years, I had seen lots of things that were surprising and terrible. I thought then that nothing surprised me anymore. But this was unbelievably astonishing. How in the world had I missed this? How long had she been snorting cocaine while caring for my children? Is this why she was always so cheerful and upbeat at the end of a long day? My thoughts were wild and angry. How could she do this? How did I miss this? How long had it been going on? Had the children seen her snorting cocaine? It hit me like no other surprise ever had. And I felt guilty for missing her drug use. I never had a clue.

After she recovered from the episode, I fired her. She begged me to allow her to continue working, doing some housecleaning. I let her clean house for a while, but by then the children were scared of her, and I had to let her go. Such a sad and strange story about a sweet lady with a dreadful drug problem. I am sorry to admit that I have no idea what happened to her.

Four years into our sojourn in Arkansas, my husband and I began to renegotiate a plan for our marriage. We were not getting along well, and I was desperate for some changes. He was traveling every few months to major cities like Chicago, San Francisco, and New York for his work with the residency education program. Even though I was no longer clinically depressed, I continued to be unhappy at work and was absent from home with too much night call. Phillip complained that I was in a perpetual bad mood, implying that it was simply my choice. I could not comprehend that Abraham Lincoln quote, "People are about as happy as they make up their mind to be." He was professionally up while I was clearly down and floundering. Thus, began our first endeavor to correct the situation in which we found ourselves—an unhappy marriage and an imbalanced partnership.

His best friend kept telling him, "If Momma ain't happy, ain't nobody happy," and he finally listened. We tried weekly date nights, and sometimes we had fun together, but usually we ended up talking about my frustrations with work. Although the call schedule improved slightly as we hired more attendings, the way Doc B. managed his division did not change. We began to seriously discuss our problems—personal and work-related—and I told him that if we did not move, I would move by myself. I do not think that I would have gone through with such an escape, but I considered it. And that was the moment when we both began to search for other things to do professionally.

Despite accomplishing some good QI work with ROP and establishing a successful milk bank and breastfeeding program, I continued to be disappointed with my academic progress. I published a few more papers, but my grant application for the NICHD neonatal network was not accepted. Taking care of sick babies no longer felt as rewarding as it once was, and I assumed that leaving the NICU would fix this. So, I took the advice of my critical care colleague, and applied for a job as medical director of QualChoice, a small HMO (Health Maintenance Organization) affiliated with the medical school. This position would allow me to remain on the UAMS faculty and retain my benefits.

So, for my last two years in Little Rock I took a detour, changed course, and worked as the medical director for QualChoice, an organization created in 1994 to provide health benefits for Arkansas companies, families, and individuals. QualChoice coordinated and managed care for the university's self-funded health plan, in an attempt to control costs generated by the university faculty physicians and other contracted providers. I relaxed into the easy work of reviewing cases and attending meetings, assessing appeals, and visiting with groups of physicians. Those manageable eight-to-five office hours were so easy, and the training meetings for physician executives convened in scenic locations, such as Vail and Beaver Creek, Colorado, were so relaxing. Finally, I had an easy life, too.

At that time, in 1995, most HMOs were medical insurance groups that provided health services for a fixed annual fee. These organizations coordinated services with providers (hospitals, doctors, and therapists) on a prepaid basis. HMOs covered costs of care given by contracted doctors who treated patients in accordance with the HMO's guidelines in exchange for a steady supply of patients. HMOs required members to select a primary care doctor (PCP) who served as "gatekeeper" for specialty services. HMOs had some good features, such as covering preventive services like immunizations, well-baby checkups, mammograms, and annual physicals. In addition, HMOs did a good job with case management and disease management, assigning seasoned nurses to work with patients and providers to control services (and therefore costs) for complex diseases such as diabetes, asthma, and cancer.

I found the QualChoice data review to be interesting, especially since we compared all our local (statewide) numbers for diagnoses and procedures to national standards. Arkansas was not a healthy state when I practiced there. The rates of obesity and diabetes were high. Smoking and heart disease were common and teen pregnancy was a huge problem. These numbers were fascinating, but a large part of me felt like a traitor. Explaining negative judgments to other physicians, judgments that were based on standardized national guidelines for care, and literally out of my hands, was uncomfortable. I had defected to the inner workings of an organization that tried to influence physician practice patterns by controlling reimbursements for their panel of patients. It was an eye-opening experience.

Looking back now, I realize that my time in Little Rock was a true valley in my life of many mountains, a place of profound pain and disappointment. I learned quite a bit about clinical practice patterns, quality improvement, and HMOs there, and my husband and I were forced to confront our marital struggles head-on. But even more, my time there showed me that I had enough grit and self-discipline to endure. I had resilience enough to try new things, and I grew to understand that the love of my children grounded me during this period of stress and struggle. During that time when I learned so much about resilience, my children were the precise spot to which I was secured while adapting to my life's transitions. They were the touch point from which I made progress.

Chapter 10

DOG BITES AND DYSLEXIA

Anne was only four years old when we relocated to Little Rock, and she immediately began to tell me, "Mommy, I'm scared of robbers and burglars." Her fears were so disturbing that when she awoke in the night, she padded downstairs to our bedroom and made herself a little pallet of blankets on the floor next to me. When I awoke in the morning, there she would be nestled under her pink blanket right at my beside. For several months she did this. Besides, she had another good reason to get out of her bed—nocturnal enuresis, or nighttime bed-wetting. Anne had been toilet-trained since age three but had never been dry at night. Our lovely little daughter would wake up during the night with cold, soggy sheets, and wet pajamas, get out of her bed, put on a new pair of panties and a T-shirt, and come down to our room with her pillow and blanket for comfort. Occasionally she did not get up out of bed, instead she rolled over in her twin bed to a position nearer the wall where there was a dry spot. She never complained. We gave her lots of reassurance and understanding, knowing that this was a normal childhood condition.

Bed-wetting is a normal developmental phenomenon. Lots of children with perfectly normal kidneys and bladders wet the bed. Sometimes stressful events, like becoming a big sister, starting a new school, or sleeping away from home, can trigger bed-wetting. Poor darling Anne suffered through all three at once. When I discussed this with my new pediatrician, he suggested treatment with medication, but my pediatric nephrologist husband objected vehemently to this advice. He could be very stubborn about some things, and his refrain was, "It's normal; let it run its course." We knew not to fuss about this. Nevertheless, there were mornings when I sighed heavily as I gathered up the wet sheets and headed downstairs to the laundry room.

Children do not need to feel guilty or embarrassed about a normal developmental phase, but this one affected her friendships. As she grew older, she was embarrassed about having fewer opportunities for sleepovers at friends' houses. Luckily, her best friend's physician mother kept a plastic sheet on the extra bunk bed where Anne slept when she was there and said nothing about the wet sheets, so Anne always felt safe sleeping at their house.

For fully six months after our move Anne expressed fears of robbers and began to outwardly show nervousness. Without complaining, she often carried a worried look on her precious face, furrowed brow, and all. Sometimes before her bedtime, we walked around the house together, checking all the windows and doors. She started to bite her fingernails, and I learned sometime later that her new preschool teacher, Miss Marty, allowed Anne to sit on her lap each day for the first two months of preschool. Miss Marty was a tender hearted, middle-aged woman who adored teaching young children. What a wonderful and understanding preschool teacher (although I do wish she had told me this). As Anne settled down and learned to roller-skate, she began to feel comfortable and act well.

Miss Jean Anthony, a wise old woman who founded the Anthony School, believed that children who roller-skated became empowered at an early age. In that school, we saw two- and three-year old children happily skating up and down the halls on carpet. Anne was physically coordinated and skated well on the gym linoleum floor. She was also riding her bike proficiently at age four. Later that next summer she learned to swim surprisingly well, at age five. The neighborhood lifeguard, Carrie, was herself a tan, blonde collegiate swimmer and she personally supervised Anne's swimming lessons. Anne loved to hear Carrie squeal her approval, yelling "Great legs, look at those legs." Anne learned to swim real strokes, both freestyle and backstroke, and one year later, at age six, she was swimming butterfly. Her prowess with swimming gave her huge confidence in everything else. Although she continued to wet the bed until she was nine years old, we heard nothing more about robbers.

At age six, David had been identified as "gifted and talented" in Houston. Readjusting him from a Montessori school to a traditional classroom did not go smoothly. David was tall and lanky, a brunette boy with expressive blue eyes, big buck teeth, and a mischievous grin. He tended to act goofy. In Little Rock we attempted to place him into a class of the brightest kids. His repeat testing in Little Rock at age seven confirmed that he was quite bright. Miss Marty performed several hours of standardized testing to confirm this, but she would not relinquish his IQ number, instead said, "He's a smart little boy." His new teacher, a Miss Puckett, not inexperienced but unusually high strung, was intolerant of his impulsive and immature behaviors. She fretted about him quite a lot and was convinced that he had attention deficit hyperactivity disorder (ADHD). One day she called to inform me that he had executive brain dysfunction, a condition she had just noticed.

David was not hyperactive, and he could focus, but his work was a mess. His room at home was a mess. He liked to tinker with different things—Legos, switches, cords, pieces of metal and wire—and create contraptions and tangled messes. Unfortunately, there was not a gifted and talented program in our small private school, nor was there one at the public school in our neighborhood. (Internet-based curricula for gifted kids did not materialize until the early 2000s.) The best we could do was enroll David into after-school programs and let him read whatever interested him. Later that year, when we had him formally evaluated for ADHD, the child psychologist told us unequivocally that he did not have ADHD, nor did not need medication. He remarked, "Your son is impulsive, that's all."

Remember his poking other children? Well, that recurred around second grade. The teacher's note that came home reporting your child poking another in the eye was far more traumatic than the one that was sent home reporting biting at age three. Traumatic and embarrassing, indeed. David was taught to use the

"Super Solver," a five-part solution tool that enabled him to think of better ways to act before he hit, pushed, or poked someone. At home we had calendars with stickers and charts with gold stars. He wrote me daily messages in his scratchy, left-handed style, "Hey Mom, I had a five-sticker day today. And I love you." Five stickers meant his best behavior. Third grade progressed along without incident.

By the fourth grade he was taking computers apart and putting them together again alongside Mr. Bobo, the jovial, middle-aged computer teacher. Len Bobo was a heavyset, bald man who laughed a lot and delighted in teaching children about computers. David came home speaking of motherboards and other electronic pieces about which we were clueless. Computer fun occurred after-school and in a summer computer camp. David and Mr. Bobo enjoyed their time together, and in 1994 they finally convinced us to purchase our first home computer. We had delayed buying one since my good friend, Carol, a special education teacher, told me to withhold computer games from my gifted child or else he would "slip away into never ending computer fun."

Mrs. Smith was the consummate elementary school teacher, a tall, stout woman with neatly coiffed gray hair. She kept our son, and her other students, engaged as if she was conducting a fine orchestra. She reported to us that he was ready for more challenging work than fifth grade would offer. Against our better judgment, we allowed David to skip the fifth grade. The school principal, also a consummate educator, and Mrs. Smith persuaded us that the fifth grade would be a boring repeat of fourth, and that the sixth-grade teacher was experienced and would task him appropriately. Unfortunately, she did not. Not only was he not challenged, but also, he was bullied by the older boys. One tough, skateboarder boy picked on David incessantly. That child's parents were going through a divorce, and seemingly unresponsive to my pleas to attempt to control their son.

David continued to play with computers and took up filming his sisters and their friends with our home movie camera. Altogether, the kids put on "the Okra Show," dressed in costumes, played out interviews with guests, and had a ball. After sixth grade, David attended a summer "brain camp" at the University of Central Arkansas, in Conway. This university program permitted graduate students and their faculty to study the effects of gifted and talented curricula on children. As we excitedly moved in his things and made his bed, it felt much like outfitting a dorm room for an incoming college freshman. David and the other children lived in the dorms for two weeks, all the while supervised by college student mentors. Afterwards, I felt relieved that he liked brain camp, identified with other bright, nerdy kids, and did not become homesick.

Our Houston backyard was small and usually flooded after rainstorms. In Little Rock, our large, grassy backyard filled with tall pine trees was a wonderful gift. Pinnacle Mountain could be viewed from our back deck. We constructed a swing set, monkey bars and climbing fort, located within a pit of soft pea gravel. Our children and all the neighborhood kids had fun there, and I relished playing with my children, whether outside or elsewhere, whenever possible. I taught the kids to play Wiffle ball and to pitch and catch. On hot summer afternoons they ran through the sprinklers and delighted in belly-flopping on the Slip and Slide. Kids often gathered deep in our back yard on this large boulder they called "the Rock," their special place. In late summer, we picked blackberries from the bushes growing wild in that lovely backyard. David and his father built a lop-sided, triangular, wooden tree fort between three pines, deep in the yard. My children rode tricycles and bikes in our neighborhood cul-de-sac, and we frequented the neighborhood swimming pool just two blocks down the street. So many summer hours were spent happily in our backyard or down at the pool. For me, child's play was then, and still is, therapeutic. It remains a favorite way to fill up my cup.

Laura, our third child, was the easiest baby and toddler ever. She slept through the night at two weeks of age and breastfed until she turned one. She was a chubby, cheerful toddler with green eyes and delightful, sandy blonde ringlets. Laura had no issues with behavior, tantrums, sleeping, fears, or bed-wetting. Nothing. Often wearing nothing but a diaper, she chased her older siblings around and attempted to do everything they did. They often dressed her in costumes for the Okra Show. Her siblings and the neighborhood girls doted over her. She was everyone's baby, and her nickname was "Baby Wawa," after the way she pronounced her own name.

One warm Sunday afternoon, when Laura was three, a myriad of kids was playing outside. I was about ten feet away from Laura and the other children were more spread out, some on bicycles, and some walking. Sara, the neighbor's dog, was a black and white, hyper Springer Spaniel. In one quick moment, Laura held out her hand to pet Sara. She was arm's length from the dog's face, and instantly, Sara nipped at Laura's face. In my mind's eye, there was blood everywhere and it appeared as if her upper lip had been filleted open. I grabbed Laura and ran screaming to our house. My husband helped me to assess the damage and settle down. I was frantic and terribly upset, as I recollected one instance that Sara had briefly growled at Laura while she licked a popsicle on the back deck. My husband calmly paged the pediatric plastic surgeon on call and requested that he meet us in the emergency room.

Two hours later the surgeon placed fifteen blue, plastic, thread-like stitches in her upper lip, while Laura laid asleep on a table next to me. Thankfully, that surgeon was patient and used only a sedative and local anesthetic (numbing agent). That afternoon the surgeon told me about another little boy he saw recently whose cheek had been bitten by a dog. He told me, "That dog took a chunk out of that child's cheek and swallowed it." He was just trying to make me feel better, but I still felt miserable and guilty somehow. We took Laura home to rest and heal, and it took several days for me to calm down.

Our nice neighbors, the ones who owned Sara, the biting dog, were concerned but nothing more. Nevertheless, we believed that dogs that bite children should be put down—euthanized. That is every pediatrician's mantra. This family did not want to do that, and my husband and I were hurt and angry. Our neighbors finally proffered their pet to another family who lived on a farm out of town. Laura's lip healed nicely and afterwards she was, unbelievably, unafraid of large dogs. At the time, I felt awful about that incident. I had been a mere ten feet away, had witnessed the bite, and the blood gushing in agonizing slow motion, yet I was helpless to intervene. Moreover, I had witnessed Sara's brief growl at her on another day, yet I was unable to predict her biting my baby.

On a happier note, the neighborhood swim team was a godsend—and Anne was a swimming star. David tried his best but was too uncoordinated to swim competitively. Soccer was not a fit for him either. He could run fast but could not run and kick at the same time. In fact, David was more like "Ferdinand the Bull" (from the children's book by Munro Leaf) in that he would stand out in the field and look around, noticing everything except the soccer ball approaching him. In contrast, Anne was an incredibly good athlete. By age seven she joined a club swim team and swam daily for several years. In fact, we traveled all around the state attending her weekend swim meets and helping her gather up her cache of ribbons and trophies.

My husband and I both delighted in watching her swim—and win—especially at butterfly. She stood poolside, with her slim and fit, little eight-year-old body in her skintight blue, team racing suit, with her hair tucked into her white swim cap, LASERS written on one side of the cap, and ANNE on the other. She pulled on those blue goggles and pressed the heels of each hand into her eyes to ensure the goggles were tight. Then she would bravely climb up onto the starting block and off she went. She was a sight to behold, swimming like a little dolphin. That is when I first began to think of Anne as perfect. I was contented in seeing her as a happy child, one who felt love, and one with good self-esteem. I even imagined her going to the Olympics one day. Surely all mothers indulge in this sort of dreaming of triumph or success for their children.

As we traveled around Arkansas, I found it to be quite beautiful, and geographically much like South Carolina where I grew up. We visited the Ozark Folk Center in Mountain View when Laura was eight months old. I remember discreetly nursing her while seated at the table in a local diner, and the family nearby almost fell out of their chairs, staring at me. Their chubby toddler was sitting in his highchair holding the nipple of a half empty bottle of formula in his teeth and shaking his head back and forth. Later that year in Little Rock, as I waited in the checkout line at Target one afternoon, someone bluntly asked me if Laura was my granddaughter. They seemed quite surprised when I informed them that she was, in fact, my daughter. I must have looked especially old and tired that day. Laura had naturally curly hair when she was a toddler, and on two other occasions, I was queried outright, "Do you perm her hair?" Each time I felt affronted and wondered how anyone might think that I would create one of those "toddlers and tiaras" kind of child. Later on, I learned that some mothers do.

Laura, at age four, exhibited no interest in books like her siblings had shown. She had trouble learning shapes, letters, and numbers. One day, watching her quietly looking at a book by herself, happily turning the pages, I noticed that the book was upside down. The school had sent home some small, laminated phonics flip cards for practice learning rhyming words, like "hop," "bop," and "pop" or "bad," "sad," "dad," but she couldn't work them. Rhyming words defied her. She saw lowercase b's as d's and mixed up lots of other letters. In her mind, letters and their sounds did not connect. She had trouble learning new words and her speech development was delayed as well.

This situation, and this condition, was brand-new to me, so I shifted into supermom overdrive. I read papers, interrogated experts, and scheduled appointments to assess her speech, hearing, and vision. Her hearing was fine; her speech was delayed but "within the range of developmental norms." I was told that she did not have an auditory perceptive disorder, as some dyslexic children do. Her vision tested normal, too. Nevertheless, I carted her off to see this dyslexia "doctor" in Memphis who fitted her for reading glasses, which essentially magnified the words, just like bifocals. We used color-tinted plastic overdrafts to enhance her word reading skills. These were touted as special aids yet did not prove to be that helpful. Nonetheless, Laura was happy to wear her pretty, rainbow-colored glasses; they must have made her feel special.

She had no trouble interacting with her peers. Her fine motor skills were not the best which caused her trouble with writing. But her gross motor skills were normal. In fact, she was physically active and rambunctious. We decided to have her learning disability formally tested, and the testing showed that her intellect was well above average, but because of her dyslexia she scored two years behind. I felt reassured to learn that while dyslexia impacts learning, it's not a problem of intelligence. By five years of age Laura was coping better and capable of doing most kindergarten work. However, her concept of numbers and math was worse than that for letters and reading. Moreover, telling time remained elusive to her.

Laura had been a ten-pound, healthy full-term, newborn. My pregnancy was normal, without gestational diabetes. She had no hypoglycemia (low blood sugar) after birth. So, I floundered to explain her dyslexia and learning disabilities. I knew that the premature infants I cared for and sent home from the hospital were at unusually high risk for learning disabilities. In fact, the smallest babies had the highest risk. So, I was troubled about what caused Laura's brain to develop in this atypical way. No one could explain to me, nor could I determine a cause from all my reading about dyslexia. So, she learned to cope and struggled to learn. We practiced and we practiced. She had to work twice as hard as her siblings to learn something new, especially spelling. She often came home from school, tears streaming down her cheeks, complaining of being "stupid," and it broke my heart each time. I told her that she was not stupid, but that her brain was just wired differently. That became our family mantra: "Your brain is just wired differently."

During our Little Rock years, we always gathered for family meals when my husband and I were both at home. We sat down for dinner around one table, and TV was not allowed. My husband found cooking pleasurable and from a young age, David delighted in learning to cook by standing on a stool beside him in the kitchen. This worked out nicely because I distinctly disliked cooking. My children can count on two hands the limited number of dishes that I made for them. On Friday nights when I was off, we piled into the old, gray Ford Bronco and went to Shorty Smalls or the Purple Cow for burgers and those famous, creamy, purple milkshakes. Family dinners were a special time for us all, sometimes loud, sometimes argumentative, but always happy.

To keep our household running efficiently, my husband and I divided up the labor. He did all the grocery shopping and cooking, and prepared school lunches for the kids each morning, while the rest of us ate breakfast together. He also drove the children to school each day in the Bronco. He enjoyed allowing our children to accompany him to the grocery store, where they sampled healthy fruits and vegetables, tried various cheeses, and tasted other interesting foods. For us, this distribution of duties seemed like an equitable split. I took care of teacher meetings, school counselor meetings, pediatrician appointments, dentist and orthodontist appointments, birthday parties, sleepovers, play dates, gifts for other children, volunteering at the school, permission slips, swim team parties, teacher and coach gifts, costumes, sports uniforms, music lessons, and anything having to do with the nannies. Just a typical mother's list.

The Little Rock Athletic Club, a nearby fitness center, offered something for each of us. My husband and I left work early, when we could, to exercise and use the equipment there. Or, we went there as a family on the weekend. During those years, we both learned to appreciate the importance of regular exercise.

It was an effective way to control stress, stay in shape, and refill my cup. They offered childcare for the little ones, as well as sports camps, and games programs for the older kids. I tried to exercise two or three days a week when I was not on-service in the NICU, and I noticed that exercise was a superb down-regulator of my stress. Anne was there swimming every afternoon, and I relished catching a glimpse of her at swim practice. One Saturday when Anne was around nine years old, she wandered off with another little girl to play racket ball. Where they got the racquets and balls I will never know. But the next thing we knew, Anne turned up crying with a black-and-blue, swollen, broken nose. Her friend had accidentally hit her in the face with a racquet. We were off to the emergency room again. In my motherhood life it was always live and learn: Unsupervised children can do just about anything to hurt themselves.

While working in Little Rock, somehow, I carved out the time to make costumes for my children. Sewing them gave me a sense of accomplishment and pride. (My mother had taught me to sew when I was a teenager, and it stuck.) There were simple ghost and witch costumes for Halloween, and a royal blue king's cape edged in white fur that David wore in a school play. My greatest sewing achievement for Laura was a Harry Potter robe, with a hood, made of scarlet and silver satin. When I completed all those, I was still working full-time, and looking back now, I cannot imagine how I finished it all. And I began stitching again when the children were away or napping. Once again, I recognized that mindless needlework, like crewel and counted cross-stitch, was relaxing.

However, I continued to compare myself to other working mothers and ask myself how they got it all done. My critical care colleague always seemed perfectly prepared with her two children. I remember the year that she volunteered to be room mother, a huge job in any school. David and her son were in the same fourth grade class. Deidra was ultra-organized and known as a micro-manager at work. At the start of the school year she distributed a spreadsheet on which was listed each child in the class and their mother's name, phone number, each child's birthday, and all the upcoming holidays for the school year. She preemptively assigned each mother one holiday with a note indicating what to bring for that specific party—cookies, cake, drinks, decorations, or whatever. None of the usual means of willy-nilly signing-up to bring something. When I saw this, I was dumbfounded. Still later that year I witnessed her "helping" our two sons with their science project on Sunday afternoons. I cannot recall what it was about, but I am certain they won first place. My friend probably never yelled at her children, but I would not be her kind of mother.

We celebrated the fact that Anne also experienced Mrs. Smith as her fourth-grade teacher. At the end of the year, Mrs. Smith allowed the children to vote on superlative awards for one another. She told them that each child had a positive strength and they must find something good about each classmate to recognize. They convened for a party in the school library, with some moms sitting on chairs observing, and all the children spread out, sitting on the floor. I watched as Mrs. Smith handed out certificates for most athletic girl, and smartest girl, and friendliest girl. When every category had been awarded and my child had nothing, she saw me begin to outwardly fret. Then Mrs. Smith winked at me and called out, "The final award is for "best all-around girl" and that goes to Anne Berry." My feelings of love and delight were explosive.

A favorite memory of our time in Little Rock was Mother's Day Eggs Benedict breakfast-in-bed. My husband created this annual tradition, and all our children participated. He taught David to poach eggs and make hollandaise sauce, and the girls carefully gathered good china, pretty placemats, and napkins, and decorated the tray with little flowers and bowls of colorful fruit sprinkled with powdered sugar. Then, all together, they entered my bedroom carefully carrying my breakfast tray. The girls presented me with wonderful cards lovingly crafted at school. One year, David proudly gifted me with a two-inch square of gold tile made into a brooch, with a pin glued onto its back. On the tile front he spelled out SUPER MOM with sequins and glitter. That treasured homemade brooch still dwells safely within my bedside table.

We were strict parents about some things. There were no guns in our home; David had only one or two toy guns. We did not allow a trampoline, either. They were known to be dangerous and cause spinal cord injuries. At work, we heard about dreadful, three-wheeler rollovers causing life-threatening head injuries or deaths. Two of the boys on our street rode them around and tried to look cool. David knew without asking that he would never get one. My husband came home from the hospital one day and sadly described to me a girl he saw in the PICU whose hair was caught in the motor of a go-cart. He said, "She was scalped." We told David simply that go-carts were dangerous. Knowing which playthings threaten children's safety, and being committed to prohibiting them, parents like us—careful pediatricians—must undoubtedly seem strict compared to normal parents.

Maternal growth occurred slowly for me, unfolding throughout the years, and increased with the number of my children. Along the way, you are confronted with events and challenges previously unseen. Before leaving Houston, Patty, my friend, and fellow healer, warned me that mothering three children was much more onerous than two. She and her husband often recounted struggles with their three teens during our group meetings. She advised two things: actively filling up my cup and finding ways to strengthen my marriage. She told me that a solid marriage was crucial to good parenting. So, during the Arkansas years, while chasing around three kids, I struggled to learn how to be good, or at least better, to myself. And Phillip and I scheduled some date nights. I tried guided meditation however, it did not work for me—I could not concentrate with a little one tapping at the door. Laura remembers my listening to calming Enya tapes in the car while driving to errands and appointments. I remember listening to classic rock tunes from the 1970s, and because she knows the words to all of these songs, I'm probably correct.

Regular exercise became a prime tool for controlling my stress. When I worked at QualChoice, David and I began running in our hilly neighborhood, but workouts at the Athletic Club were my favorite, and I loved soaking in the hot tub afterwards. I continued to learn how to relax and refresh when I had some time off. On Saturday mornings post-call, the girls and I took bubble baths together. Our master bathroom had an elevated Jacuzzi tub. We filled it with hot water, added liquid bubble bath, and turned up the jets. The bubbles grew into something magically playful, sometimes so high that they covered up three-year-old Laura. Bubbles spilled over the side of the tub and onto the floor, as we just laughed and laughed. I never minded the bubble mess. Playing together in a warm bubble bath was wonderful, one great means of filling up my cup.

It was during our years in Arkansas that I revised my personal goal to be a good-enough mother. I had long since abandoned the notion of being a perfect mother. For me, there was no such thing. My husband and my psychiatrist, the one who aided me through my depression, each tried to convince me that even though I was not a perfect mother, I was usually a good-enough mother. I gave my children hugs and kisses, sang to them, and read books with them for hours and hours. I told them that I loved them. I helped with homework, and spelling, and facilitated their projects. I tried desperately to peel away from work and be there for all their school plays, productions, and class parties. I was present in their lives whenever I was not at work.

Nonetheless, I was absent often during those first four years in Little Rock. In the beginning, I worked excessively, was away overnight on-call at least twice each week and spent too many ten-hour days in the hospital. This schedule commonly brought out the worst in me. In the early years, when I was continually stressed, I remember yelling at my children often, especially David, since he was so lackadaisical with schoolwork. When I was overwhelmed by the chaos of three kids at home, I shouted too much. I especially fussed at David when he acted passive and lazy. Once, when David was ten years old, sitting at his messy desk tinkering or dreaming, not completing an overdue book report, I slapped him. There it was again—my unacceptable, juvenile, bad-mother behavior. When my abnormal conduct recurred that day, I left the house, trudged through the woods for nearly an hour, ruminated on my problem, and felt horrible. I had stooped to physical punishment, again. How disheartened I felt to realize that my problem persisted. My aberrant behavior had been stuffed down deep but was not yet gone.

Chapter 11

DELIVERANCE

fter six years of living and working in Little Rock, my husband and I
decided to save our marriage and move to Austin, Texas. It was 1997.
I joined an Austin neonatology practice that consisted of nine men,
five of whom I had trained with in Houston and knew well. (Three of us trained
as fellows together, and two were fellows when I was on faculty at TCH.) It was
easy to get hired since they knew me well and they needed another neo. This
time, I was wiser and chose to begin my new role slowly, working part time at a
low-risk women's delivery center in town. It was the perfect way for me to ease
into the Austin medical scene, and it balanced well with my duties as a mother
of three children now spread out in three different schools. At that time, my
children were seven, ten, and thirteen years old.

Working with nurse practitioners at the Renaissance delivery center was
fun, although "part time" for me turned out to be thirty-five hours a week.
The NNPs and I got along well and felt a sense of comradery. The center was
beautifully appointed, comfortable, and spacious. We took care of healthy term
babies, some larger preterm babies, a few babies with low blood sugars, mostly
infants of diabetic mothers, and the occasional crash C-section for fetal distress.

In general, the NNPs attended deliveries, and I supervised. However, one of the premier obstetricians—the one who helped create this "hospital-like birthing center"—proved to be a challenge. A fellow redhead, she insisted on delivering anyone there she wanted to, low-risk or not. The center was designed for low-risk deliveries since we did not offer intermediate care nursery services. She enjoyed sneaking in moms with mild pre-eclampsia, diabetic moms, and moms in preterm labor. She and her partners also allowed water births there, despite the current evidence against their safety. That year at the Renaissance, I plucked two cold babies from their water bath births and, interestingly, fielded lots of questions about marijuana use during breastfeeding.

I will never forget examining the baby of a celebrity's granddaughter. Her grandchild presented with a heart murmur on day two and, on day three, I opined that it was probably a VSD, a ventricular septal defect, and talked with the family about this. I made a referral to the pediatric cardiologist for a check-up and ultrasound the following week and called an update to her pediatrician. While examining the baby prior to discharge and reviewing my typical discharge instructions, I commented on her beautiful name, Claudia. When I asked where it came from, the baby's grandmother stood up, looked slightly offended, and said, "Well, my mother was named Claudia long before she became Lady Bird." I felt so stupid and rightfully apologized. Thank goodness, the baby did well and her VSD closed spontaneously.

There was one unforgettable, tragic moment at the Renaissance Center while I practiced there. A young pediatrician came in for vaginal delivery of her first baby, and everything went perfectly until her baby boy refused to turn pink. He had a good heart rate and breathed vigorously, but as his color changed from blue to dark purple around ten minutes of age, they summoned me in to assess him. The little guy had a loud heart murmur and, upon checking his chest X-ray, his heart appeared as a classic "egg on a string," diagnostic for a severe congenital heart defect called transposition of the great vessels. We quickly transferred the baby to the Children's Hospital in Austin for a palliative heart catheterization procedure. It was heartrending to watch this young pediatrician tearfully and courageously deal with this unexpected catastrophe. Once again, thinking—it could have been me.

After moving to Austin, my children each needed various types of assistance with settling in. Fortunately, we chose a new home in a neighborhood with excellent public schools. My part-time work allowed me the free time necessary to meet with new teachers, counselors, and coaches. Within twelve months, however, everyone seemed happy, and since the kids appeared to be well-adjusted, I chose to return to full-time work in the NICU. In retrospect, that was what my mother would have called "jumping out of the frying pan and into the fire."

It was a culture change, to say the least—not so much the NICU practice, but the partners themselves. Each of the nine men in my new practice was married to a stay-at-home mom. This neonatology practice was busy, and the NICU at Seton Medical Center was well run, but when I joined the group, they had a peculiar way of sharing their workload, taking night call, and dividing up their time off. They worked three weeks of days, with shared call on those weekends, then worked one week of nights, and then had one week off. This schedule rolled along regardless of their other needs. Personal obligations were scheduled during their week off. I was plugged into this rotation and told to take vacation when my week off turned up. About six months into this new full-time schedule, I grew brave enough and pleaded for scheduling vacation in advance so that my husband and I could share time off together. They were reluctant to change just to accommodate me.

Another six months passed, and I pressed my luck to address another problematic issue: starting daily morning rounds at 7 a.m. This established practice of all males had been doing that for years, but I insisted that doing so prevented me from seeing my children before they left for school each day. I pleaded that I didn't have a wife at home to care for their needs and get them all dressed, fed, and out of the door before my leaving for work at 6:30 a.m. Of course, I did have a husband who performed all these parental tasks, but I wanted to do those things, too. I argued convincingly for beginning morning rounds at 8 a.m. After some grumbling and much discussion, they agreed to the change. A few months later, several of them told me that they liked the modification and appreciated seeing their own children before the school day started. It was my first female doctor victory.

The Seton Hospital NICU was full of routine preemies as well as complex neonatal cases; it was both busy and challenging, in a good way. About two years into my full-time position in Austin, we began to interview young neonatologists to join the practice. In a group business meeting, one of the more senior partners made a short but heartfelt "speech." David was usually a man of few words, but this time he stood up and explained that he wanted to hire another woman because he thought "having a woman in the practice had brought some positive changes." I was quietly astonished and extremely pleased. I sat there in that meeting genuinely happy, smiling inwardly, while we decided to choose another woman to fill our new position. Serena was an energetic, young neonatologist with small children who turned out to be just as opinionated as me about schedules and flexibility for raising children. That felt like another victory.

Amid our caring for sick babies, we would all pause and gather for biweekly business meetings. There was rarely a time during which all the neonatologists could attend, but we tried. Our meetings, convened in the comfortable library conference room outside of the NICU, were supposed to start at 8 a.m. There was one partner who always bounded in ten or twelve minutes late. The medical director typically started the meeting, then backtracked to fill in what the tardy physician had missed, thereby penalizing those of us who arrived on time. As an on-time kind of person, I found this irritating. Our meetings were usually peaceful discussions of practice guidelines, clinical data reviews, or deliberations about problems with NNPs or residents. Issues with L&D policies or obstetricians were also reviewed. I appreciated having a medical director who was organized and thorough— and I never once regretted leaving Little Rock.

One unlucky volunteer was nominated to generate and submit the schedule for the whole practice—workdays on, days off, weekend call, vacations, holidays, and such. My second year there, I volunteered to create the group schedule and did so for many years so that I could claim specific days off to synchronize with my husband's schedule. Creating and adjusting the schedule, with pencil on paper, took me several tedious hours every month. Years later, one of my younger female partners took control of the schedule using a software program that seemed complicated to me, but it allowed doctors to "switch" with one another online without bothering her.

We relocated to Austin in December 1997 when David was in middle school and Anne was in fifth grade. From the onset, Anne was furious with our move. She begged us to allow her to stay in Little Rock and live with her teacher. Despite her teacher's offer, of course, we said no. One day, after only two months in Austin, she shouted, "You have ruined my life," and punched her father in the abdomen. The previous year, Anne was very happy. She was notably a good student, a great friend, and a social butterfly. Losing the stability of her school friends, teachers who adored her, and her swim team coach and teammates was too much for her. She began to sleep on the floor next to my bed again, this time on a hardwood floor. She expressed fears of robbers again, but now I know that she was just plain scared, and her ten-year-old brain didn't know how to express that.

In looking back on Anne's trials during that transition, I default to my "bad mother" tape. It's the tape that says, "Why didn't I know what this meant and what I should do about it?" Why had I been so quick to think that she just needed another swim team and a new classroom full of kids? She had always made friends easily, was smart, and enjoyed swimming. In retrospect, hiring a new nanny, helping each child settle into new classrooms, and working part time left me too busy to offer Anne the extra attention she required. Perhaps my preoccupation with securing all the services that Laura needed also played a role in my not appreciating Anne's fears.

After trying out several different swim clubs during fifth grade and middle school, Anne finally found a team and a female coach that she liked and began to feel comfortable. But I distinctly remember having to sit by the pool and watch her swim many times before she could be left alone with the coach and her new teammates. It was sad to see her so frightened, but I was too impatient to give her the help she needed, and I rationalized that I was busy, and she would settle down soon enough. By the sixth grade, Anne was acting perfectly fine, but she remembers me allowing her "to look and dress nerdy" that year. Either her hair was too short, her bangs were not cool, or her clothes and shoes were wrong. Thankfully, in eighth grade she met her new best friend, Ginger, who initiated Anne into her popular clique of girls. Anne and Ginger remained best friends throughout middle school, high school, and on into college. After Anne started driving, she spent most afternoons after swim practice at Ginger's house.

Although the move to Austin had been traumatic to her early on, I always thought that Anne adapted well and continued to act like the perfect child. She was pretty, intelligent, athletic, and caring. She seemed to be a typical middle child—a quiet facilitator and peacemaker. I wanted her to grow up with good self-esteem, so I often told her, "you are perfect—just the way you are." In retrospect, I worry that my saying this contributed to her tendency toward perfectionism. Had she heard me say, "You need to *be* perfect?" While in middle school, Anne became a picky eater. In eighth grade, at age thirteen, we noticed that she pushed food around on her plate and only pretended to eat whenever she was worried about something. She simply denied being hungry. But she was fit, swimming often, and not losing any weight.

New to the school district, Laura had to be tested again, and both the school counselor and her new teacher believed that her ADHD condition required medication. We struggled with the idea of medicating our seven-year-old—so I talked to experts and reviewed several scientific papers about the effects (and side effects) of stimulant medications for ADHD. Laura was offered the Slingerland curriculum for dyslexic children in kindergarten, and it proved perfect for her. I attended many meetings with counselors, teachers, and the principal. (Surprisingly, these educators revealed that some parents prefer not to have their child medicated, much less diagnosed as learning disabled. By contrast, I saw the diagnosis as an opportunity for her to receive extra services.)

We decided to use medication, and within six months, all agreed that it helped Laura focus and learn. Fortunately, our new public school system was flush with master's degree–prepared elementary school teachers trained in the Slingerland method. This is a multisensory curriculum that involves auditory, visual, and kinesthetic-motor processing to learn letters, sounds, words, and reading. So, Laura was identified formally as a "special needs" child, and she benefited from a lot of additional accommodations and pull-out sessions during the school day. She lucked into the same skilled, patient, and loving teacher for her first and second grade classes. We found Mrs. Gadson to be easygoing, calm, and caring, and, more importantly, Laura adored her.

David, meanwhile, dropped back into the seventh grade because of impulse control and academic issues. Moving him up from fourth to sixth grade in Little Rock had been harmful to his social development. He was too young and immature to fit into the group of boys who were always a year older than him. And he had been bullied mercilessly. Upon moving to Austin, we hoped to correct our previous mistake by allowing him to drop back into seventh grade, where he would be naturally, according to his chronological age. But in December, the middle school groups were already established. In Austin, he liked school and did well academically but remained a loner for a while.

David developed a good friendship with another pleasant, geeky boy who was a year younger. They were both computer whiz kids and enjoyed tinkering, building, dissecting computers, and electronic things. They had been friends for about a year when this young man was tragically killed in an awful skiing accident. While skiing with his family, he fell on a slope, and the tip of his ski hit him squarely in the throat. This child's death was, of course, a horrific tragedy for his parents, his older brother, and for everyone at his school, including David. David talked with his father about his friend's death, and they attended the funeral together. Later, he talked to a counselor, too, which helped him cope.

One unforgettable moment occurred the year David was still thirteen. He stuck his head in my bedroom door to ask me a question. I was lying down, reading *Real Boys*, by William Pollack. Sheepishly, he asked, "Mom, is there something wrong with me?" Then he told me that when I read books all the time it made him feel as if there were something wrong with him. I was crushed. I reassured him that nothing was wrong with him, that life in middle school was hard and a big adjustment for everyone, and that he had been through a lot. I explained that I liked to read about and understand all the challenges that were going on in our lives. That day, he seemed satisfied with my answer, but it made me reconsider how not only everything we say, but also everything we do, affects our children.

During that time, the orchestra program was a godsend for David. He already knew how to play piano and read music, especially the bass clef, fairly well, so Mrs. Henderson suggested he play double bass. He turned out to be quite good at it and loved playing bass. Mrs. Henderson was an amiable, outgoing, middle-aged orchestra teacher whom all the kids liked. David continued to play bass in the orchestra for the rest of middle school. Mrs. Henderson led us, and other orchestra families, on guided summer trips through Europe when David, and later Laura, were participating in the middle-school orchestra. Mrs. Henderson was a delight to be around, always positive and joyful. This amazing teacher arranged summer trips in which the kids saw musicals, watched theater performances, heard orchestras play, visited museums, and toured. I went along on three of those wonderful trips with her group of young teens. Only once was I called on as a physician and asked to examine one of the girls to ensure that her painful stomachache was not appendicitis.

A professional colleague, a PhD psychologist, had recommended the Boy Scouts as a remedy for David's social development. Moving to Austin offered the ideal opportunity since the Catholic church nearby had a fabulous scout troop, filled with boys just like him—smart, nerdy, and eager. The Scout Master and other scouts' fathers were committed to Troop 990, but I had to convince my husband that Scouting was a good thing. He was wary of its militaristic aspects. Although my husband was usually too busy, many of the 990 dads were free on weekends and assisted the boys with their monthly campouts. For eight months of the year, these boys and dads traveled to various state parks around Texas, such as Longhorn Cavern, McKinney Falls, Inks Lake, Palo Duro Canyon, and Camp Tahuya, beautiful places near rivers and natural springs, all accessible for weekend campouts. David prepared his camping equipment by loading his large action-packer, a giant plastic tub with a secure lid for travel.

The boys made their own campsites, pitched their own tents, knotted ropes, learned how to handle hatchets and knives, started fires, cooked their own meals, and earned scads of merit badges, which I happily sewed onto his merit badge sash. These scouts exemplified being prepared. Only once was there a mishap during one of the camping trips. David was using a sharp knife and somehow cut deeply into the index finger of his right hand. This cut severed half of a tendon, and the adult leader chose to have it repaired in the small-town hospital nearby. We weren't told about this until after the fact. Thankfully, David's finger healed normally, but that incident was scary. It could have been worse.

I enjoyed getting to know all the Seton NICU nurses, and from the start most were accepting of me as the new neonatologist. My practices were similar to those of the other doctors, so fewer questions were necessary. As a group, the nurses were quite skilled, and all were big proponents of breastfeeding, one of my favorite issues. Carol was one of our best nurses, an experienced, astute NICU nurse who worked efficiently and effectively. She was one of those nurses who had a sense about things—things that were about to go wrong. She would say, "Come over here, Suze, you need to see something." Everyone in the NICU liked her; she was outgoing, cheerful, and funny. A few years into my practice in Austin, Carol was admitted to our L&D for delivery of her second child. Her pregnancy had been uneventful, and labor and delivery went smoothly. And then I was called down to see her newborn son, Andrew. He was lying quietly on the warming bed—pink, breathing well, and moving around—but as I assessed him, I sighed with recognition that he had many physical features of Down syndrome. Of course, Carol perceived something was wrong. She and I could always read each other well. When I told her my concerns, she was heartbroken and cried. Thankfully, an echocardiogram, or heart ultrasound, done a few hours later, revealed no congenital heart defect. Two days later, the DNA test confirmed Andrew's chromosomal abnormality as Trisomy 21, and Carol cried some more. She knew that this would mean lifelong mental and developmental delays for her son.

Andrew lost too much weight and became jaundiced because of poor breastfeeding. Babies with Down syndrome are notoriously ineffective at nursing. They have a weak suck and swallow, and poor tone in the muscles of their head and neck. But Carol was determined to breastfeed him and tried a silicone nipple shield to help his poor latch. In addition, a feeding tube was placed into his mouth to supplement nursing with expressed breastmilk. She was so patient with him, and after ten days, he finally learned to nurse well enough to gain weight and go home. Carol stayed home with him for three months, and when she returned to work, she seemed optimistic and appeared to be taking his diagnosis in stride.

Not quite one month back from her maternity leave, the nurse manager asked Carol to speak with a young couple who just learned of their son's unexpected diagnosis of Down syndrome. She recounted to me that she planned to tell them what to expect medically, something she was qualified to do. She remembers that first encounter this way: "When we started talking, my nurse brain shut off and my mom brain came on. We talked about our dreams for our babies, what our goals were. It was a second child for both of us. We laughed and cried and decided that we would raise our babies with Down syndrome the same way we did our first born because that's what we knew how to do and hope for the best." After that first meeting, Carol spoke individually with every new parent of a baby born with Down syndrome at our hospital, whether their baby needed NICU care or not.

Carol took the role of parental support to a whole new level, and we all counted on her expertise. Whenever new parents were reeling with the unexpected diagnosis for their baby, she could comfort them like no one else. She spoke minimally about the medical stuff and much more about their hopes and aspirations for their new baby. Carol made raising a child affected by Down syndrome look like a special gift. Some days, her son's condition made her appear more positive about her life. When Andrew was one, she and her husband split up, and she remained a single mother to Andrew and his big sister for more than twenty years.

Carol joined the Down Syndrome Association of Central Texas and ultimately became a board member. Many of the parents she had spoken with in the hospital got involved as well, and at one point seven of the twelve board members were parents she had met and talked with in the hospital. They served because they, too, wanted to raise awareness of Down syndrome and wanted all children with Down syndrome to have the same opportunities as any other child.

Throughout Andrew's young life, Carol entertained us with updates of his progress and stories of his mischief, like flushing her wallet down the toilet. He was a stubborn child, but happily attended school where his teachers thought him to be articulate. In the NICU, we celebrated with her every milestone he mastered, and for many years he participated in the Special Olympics. His favorite event is now powerlifting. Andrew graduated from high school, with a diploma, and now attends a program that provides job training and daily living skills, hoping to one day live semi-independently. He now has a job at a local café, works out at the gym, hangs out with his friends, or sits around in his skivvies playing video games—all things typical of most twenty-year-old young men.

Some years ago, I told Carol the story of how my son, David, was bullied in school. When he skipped from fourth to sixth grade, he was immature for his age. The other boys were athletic, some rough-and-tumble skateboarders, and he ended up with few friends in his new class. I told her about the class bully who was ruthless to David for several months, always mocking him. We were in the NICU, leaning against either side of a warmer, chatting, while a sleeping preemie lay nestled in a blanket between us. I shared with her that the only child who would sit with David during lunch that year was a teenager named Richard. "Richard was a sweet-tempered fourteen-year-old with Down syndrome," I said. The afternoon I told Carol my story of how Richard had befriended my son and touched our lives, we both stood there looking at each other, smiling, and crying.

Chapter 12

SETTLING IN

My husband and I adjusted differently to our new lives in private practice. He was busy as the sole pediatric nephrologist in Austin and asked to lead a small group of pediatric subspecialists. The hospital system he worked for was growing exponentially, so his group hired three to five new pediatric subspecialists each year. In this capacity, he functioned like a small pediatric department chairman. As his practice group grew quickly, its patients overflowed the tiny children's hospital here, and they began discussions of building a new children's hospital. Meanwhile, I liked all my neonatology partners and nurses in the Seton NICU but struggled to adjust to a life of constant clinical work. Initially, I did not feel appreciated in a system that rewarded reputation for patient care over research and publications. I continued to teach clinical neonatology to residents and NNPs and volunteered to present pediatric grand rounds many times. But I still missed the academic rigor of practicing in a medical school environment.

For the first fifteen years of practicing in Austin, our group was led by a medical director who was somewhat reserved, but he was extremely intelligent and thoughtful. Tom was tall, and fit, the ultimate "Ricey," so called not only for having attended Rice University but also because he was nerdy and erudite. Rice graduates generally went on to do great things, and they very often wear their college ring, a gold signet ring emboldened with RICE, their year of graduation, and the words Letters, Science, and Art. Tom was about my age; he was an unselfish and talented clinician, and everyone liked him. However, he seemed unable to put his foot down about anything and repeatedly attempted to herd us all toward consensus. Striving for consensus in my new group appeared futile some days. In general, doctors rarely agree on exactly how things should be done (for example, exactly how to feed a tiny premature baby), unless they are spelled out clearly in published, peer-reviewed and evidence-based, clinical guidelines. By this measure, our practice was typical. We were exceptional in that we discussed studies and guidelines in an effort to achieve consensus.

Our group participated in many multicenter quality improvement, or QI, projects facilitated by our employer, Pediatrix Medical Group (now known as Mednax). In so doing, our clinical data was compared to those from other NICUs within Texas and around the country, to determine best outcomes. Typically, I volunteered to participate in these projects, most likely a result of my continual efforts to be hyper-responsible and to do something scholarly. Tom convinced me that he appreciated my participation, but I was not sure that all the other group members did. I personally found the QI projects to be enlightening and invariably worthwhile. In addition, our practice's participation provided me with some authority over the data and allowed description of best practices. I saw this QI work as semi-academic since real data were gathered and actual publications were reviewed. The QI work served as a remedy to my practicing in a private practice environment.

I will never forget one group practice meeting in which I spoke out about my bias toward a specific clinical practice and reviewed not only our own data but also a recently published paper. A much younger partner—a short, bright, high-strung man only two years out of his fellowship—interrupted me and said, "Do you ever listen, or do you just talk?" In that moment I stopped, felt agonizing, searing shame, and blushed beet-red. Then I sat there quietly for the remainder of the meeting, profoundly embarrassed. No one else commented, and I did not glance up at their faces. Clearly, I had been put in my place. It turned out that this young man became, like me, another frequently outspoken, opinionated neonatologist, who cared deeply about practice patterns and clinical outcomes. Surprisingly, he and I became friends after that incident. He had trained at another large academic medical center, and I began to recognize that he was naturally trying to carve out his own voice and style of clinical practice.

All mothers generally understand the need to adjust to the different temperaments of their children. Similarly, I adjusted to a variety of personalities among my neonatology partners—some were wonderful and caring, truly excellent clinicians, but others were troublesome and refused to share the clinical workload. And there were always formidable obstetricians to deal with. Some OBs handled neonatologists as if we were residents, calling us in to a delivery at the last minute without an introduction, and others introduced us by name to their patients and actively involved us in their care and prenatal counseling. Throughout my entire practice, I continued to learn that good interpersonal relationships are crucial to any successful work environment.

I had one partner who was unexpectedly problematic. This doctor rarely stepped up to take new patients and did not volunteer to take sick twins or triplets. He tended to dump his work onto the NNPs at night; at least, that was their story. During the day, he performed the minimal amount of work to get by but was pleasant enough to everyone, and all the parents liked him. He was known for cracking odd jokes with nurses and parents. I remember one time that Tom, our medical director, confronted me about my attitude toward this physician. He had complained to Tom, who conveyed his complaint to me: "You act like you do not respect him." This was, in fact, true, and I stubbornly informed Tom that I would not pretend to respect someone who did not pull his own weight. Tom sighed loudly, knowing I would respond that way. Throughout my entire career, I never respected anyone who was lazy. On another occasion, a different partner overheard me one day, tired, grumbling about said lazy doctor, and he chimed in, "Yes, he is definitely a slacker." Fortunately, he was counseled many times, and over the years, he slowly began to improve.

By contrast, two of the physicians with whom I worked most often, for many years, seemed to me to be perfect partners. Each of these men worked diligently, was smart, even-tempered, considerate, and thoughtful. They commonly stepped up to take sick patients or help if someone was drowning. Jeff was tall, thin, and balding. He wore wire-rimmed glasses, smiled often, and was very energetic, so much so that he bounced when he walked. Jeff was reserved, however, and only offered his opinion when asked. Best of all, he was always willing to trade call, and we both liked discussing challenging patients.

David was short and thin, spirited and engaging. He looked younger than his years, much like a college kid, with a full head of black hair and a sly smile. Both Jeff and David were polite, patient, and respectful with doctors, nurses, and parents alike. Both had joined the group practice shortly after their fellowship training. They were two of the five men who built the practice that I was privileged to join. Both were well-read and comfortable listening to new ideas, and they appreciated QI work and evidence-based clinical practice guidelines. Each one voiced to me, independently, an appreciation for the volunteer work that I did with the American Academy of Pediatrics. I greatly valued their opinions and felt this was further validation of my perseverance with academic work. For years, I marveled at the fact that David routinely solved the *New York Times* Sunday crossword puzzle with an ink pen.

In later years, Jeff became my job-sharing partner. When Anne and Laura were in high school and middle school, respectively, we developed a mutually beneficial schedule in which I worked seventy-five percent of our FTE, including most nights, and he worked the other twenty-five percent, including most weekend days. Our practice styles were similar, and I felt that I could talk to him about anything—patients, parents, or personal issues. When my sister became ill with cancer, he covered for me for weeks on end, never expecting any payback. Only once in our twenty years of working together did I hear Jeff utter a derogatory comment about an obstetrician.

After attending a high-risk delivery together, we were chatting about the popular but middling, obstetrician who had delivered the baby. It irked us both that this physician frequently misled parents and offered false hope. He would deliver a sick baby, hand the baby over to us, and quickly tell the mom sweetly, "Everything will be alright." He talked in vague generalities, clearly operating under the ninety percent rule. Most of the time (in about ninety percent of deliveries), the newborn turned out completely normal. But when he ventured into predictions about that other ten percent, those with prematurity, a significant birth defect or abnormality, he entered our purview, and that confused parents. Neither one of us respected him much at all. I learned a new word the day we attended that delivery together when Jeff said, "Boy, that man is really unctuous."

During my twenty years practicing in Austin, I genuinely enjoyed working in the NICU at Seton. The nursing staff there was excellent and the equipment first-rate. The thirty-six-bed Seton NICU was always full and busy. Our NICU cared for a balanced mix of sick term babies and tiny premature infants. When the NICU was filled with a majority of extremely low birth weight premature babies, the unit felt heavy and inequitable. These tiny babies either died or lingered for many months. We cared for plenty of big babies with congenital heart disease, and thankfully there were excellent pediatric cardiologists nearby. Cardiac ultrasounds and head ultrasounds were performed in the unit for our viewing convenience. Countless babies with birth defects and chromosomal abnormalities were born in our L&D or were outborn in towns around Austin and transferred in for care. Often, we had counseled their parents beforehand during prenatal visits to the NICU. For these babies, we appreciated the help of skilled pediatric neurologists and a pediatric geneticist.

Babies born with congenital heart disease and severe birth defects requiring surgery were commonly transferred to the Children's Hospital. Whenever possible, this occurred after their mothers had seen them and recovered enough to travel. The consultants visited these babies in our NICU, and we planned together the best timing for transfer. The NICU within the Austin Children's Hospital (later transformed into Dell Children's Medical Center) took care of neonatal surgical patients and babies born with complex genetic disorders. I worked in that NICU off and on over the years, but I found those babies to be frustratingly complicated and chronic. Some stayed in that NICU for months, a few for years.

We were lucky to have exceptional pediatric surgeons at our disposal. These men and women responded to our calls no matter the time of day or night, and they were mostly pleasant to work with. Rarely did they insist that a baby be transferred before surgery was necessary. I grew especially fond of one older, like-minded, and sarcastic, pediatric surgeon with whom I shared many patients. He was exactly my age, another opinionated, industrious baby boomer, with values and a clinical approach to patients much like mine. I recall working in the NICU one Mother's Day when he came in to consult on a baby. He asked why I was on duty that day, then frowned and shook his head at my answer. On another occasion, we were chatting socially when he discovered that my husband (who he also knew and worked with) was married before, and he exclaimed, "That makes you a trophy wife!" I adored his humor and levity in the NICU.

As a rule, the NICU staff were exceptional and worked as a team to care for each patient. We dealt with many unexpected surprises, and the birth of multiples was often a challenge for us. One Sunday evening, at about 9 p.m., an obstetrician called to alert me of the impending delivery of preterm quadruplets at 28 weeks gestation. These would undoubtedly be small babies. I sighed, paused, and said, "Fine, can you please give us an hour?" He was obviously annoyed and gruff in his response, then he delivered a short speech about unnecessary delay and our unit being a tertiary care center supposedly ready for anything. I tried to be as tactful as possible—not really—and informed him that each baby needed a nurse, a respiratory therapist, and a neonatologist or NNP. We also needed to prepare four warming beds, four ventilators and at least four sets of IV equipment. Thus, for four babies we needed to have ready at delivery twelve people and a lot of equipment. He gave us the hour, plus some, before he started that C-section.

One of my favorite patients from my early years in Austin was a little girl named Jesse, who was delivered at 28 weeks gestation to highly educated parents, a psychologist mother and an anesthesiologist father. Her mother had prematurely ruptured her membranes, or PROM, at 18 weeks gestation, and the rupture did not seal over. Her mother laid in bed in our L&D for ten weeks before delivery. Sometimes with PROM, if the leak seals over and if there is adequate amniotic fluid made from the fetal urine and the placenta, the baby is not adversely affected. In Jesse's case, her mother's amniotic fluid levels remained low, so that her lung development was detrimentally affected. (Babies do need adequate amounts of amniotic fluid throughout gestation to develop their lungs normally. Babies even have fetal breathing movements throughout gestation that keep the fluid circulating.)

When Jesse was born, she was a good size for 28 weeks gestation, but she had severe pulmonary hypoplasia—underdeveloped lungs. Moreover, she required aggressive high frequency ventilation and medications to control her pulmonary hypertension, or high blood pressure in the lung arteries. The pain on her father's face when we updated him at the bedside each day was obvious. He worked in the operating room at our hospital and dropped into the NICU often before and after his shifts.

One night, about ten days into her care, I was on call, and Jesse experienced a major setback. Her oxygen needs soared to one hundred percent and she became unstable. I was terribly busy admitting tiny preterm twins, so I called in my backup call partner. David took Jesse, and I took the rest of the unit. In my mind's eye is the image of my partner standing next to her bedside and "hand bagging" her. This means that he was using a resuscitative anesthesia bag and giving her extremely rapid and strong breaths of pure one hundred percent oxygen with his hands directly—for two hours. That night he became her human ventilator. Hand bagging can be an effective, life-saving technique, and this time it worked. Jesse stabilized and returned to her ventilator at lower oxygen settings. She slowly began to get better, although she went on to develop severe bronchopulmonary dysplasia, or BPD—chronic lung disease. The dad and I really liked working together, although her mother was more difficult to get to know. She was very calm and quiet, though, and she asked good questions: Would Jesse ever be normal? Was there any brain damage? How and when would we know?

Jesse needed IV diuretics and steroids to improve her BPD, and fortunately, she had a good response to them. Arterial sticks for frequent blood gas measurements during a rapid weaning phase made her irritable and fussy, which caused her to backslide, so I placed a peripheral arterial catheter in her wrist, which her father was tickled to see us use. (Anesthesiologists often use arterial catheters to monitor blood gases and blood pressure without disturbing the patient.) That line lasted for ten days and allowed us to aggressively wean her off the ventilator. After she was extubated and receiving oxygen by nasal cannula, we began to try feeding her by mouth. However, she was a lousy feeder from the start, with an uncoordinated suck and swallow, and after several weeks of attempting to get her to feed properly without success, I recommended a gastrostomy tube, or G-tube.

This is a connection between the stomach and the outside of the abdomen into which food or formula is inserted directly, thereby bypassing the mouth.

My recommendation for the G-tube came after twelve weeks in the hospital, when she was 40 weeks "corrected" gestational age but still could not suck and swallow effectively. It was a routine time to consider this, but this father surprised me; he dug in his heels and refused. He stood at her bedside and said, "No, I'm not having it." I guessed that he felt a G-tube would mark his daughter as defective. He had probably seen other babies with neurological and chronic disease who required a G-tube. Once he refused, all we could do was to press on. It took her mother visiting for many hours each day for two more weeks to teach Jesse to feed properly, but she did it. Jesse went home on oxygen by nasal cannula and full feeds nippled from a bottle, without a G-tube.

For months afterwards, whenever I saw her father in the doctors' lunchroom, he would flip out a picture of our girl. For several more years, whenever he saw me, he gave me an update and showed me pictures. She had grown into a normal, bright, gorgeous child with no residual effects from her newborn ordeal. My partner, David, the one who had "hand bagged" her for two hours that night, died a few years back from a brain tumor. Before his death I reminded him of how he had saved Jesse's life that night. He remembered, and in his usual quiet way, just smiled at me.

Recently, I caught up with Jesse's father by email. He thanked me, and two other doctors, for our care after her birth and remembered how frightened he was during that time. He told me that Jesse was doing well, and that she was a junior at the Ann Richards School for Young Women Leaders in Austin. She excelled in debate and adored being a cheerleader. He was so proud that she was a member of the National Honor Society and looking forward to choosing a college to attend. Finally, he noted that she "wanted to go pre-med and become a neonatologist." My eyes filled with tears as I read his note and happily recalled all that we struggled through caring for her as a newborn.

In our own family, Anne seemed to thrive during middle school once her picky eating and elementary school anxieties resolved. We enjoyed many normal, happy teenage activities, such as swim team events and school trips to Europe in the summer. We had lived in Austin for seven years when Anne's eating issues recurred as a full-blown eating disorder during her most stressful year in high school, as a junior. I knew just enough about this disorder to be terrified. She seemed happy throughout the early years of high school, made good grades, and had a considerate new boyfriend each year. However, when she turned sixteen at the start of her junior year, she became captain of the high school swim team, a Teen Teaching leader, took four AP classes, and an SAT prep course. She came home from sleepover camp, having worked there as a counselor all summer, and announced, "I'm fat and need to go on a diet." At that time, she weighed about 115 pounds, which was twenty-fifth percentile for her age. And diet she did, as she began to eat very little, mostly fruit and Special K cereal.

We could not cajole her to eat. She said she was fine and denied being hungry. She withdrew from us into her bedroom upstairs, where I sadly noticed a pink sticky note on her bedside table on which was written "EAT!" Sometimes, she complained of mild epigastric pain, so I took her to the pediatrician, who opined that she had gastric acid reflux, from stress. Even though I told the doctor about her eating problems, she instructed me not to worry and to give her antacid medication. The pediatrician did not think this was an eating disorder. To this day, I remain disappointed in her inability to diagnose Anne's condition, or to even discuss the possibility early on.

That fall, Anne lost about twelve pounds and continued to pretend to eat. It wasn't until Ginger's mother and I talked one evening in the fall that I finally understood what was going on. I called to ask her what she thought was bothering Anne. Ginger's mother told me bluntly, "Anne is not eating—not at our house, not at your house, and not at school." I was dumbstruck. This was early anorexia, and I was horrified. (In the back of my mind was the image of Karen Carpenter lying in a hospital bed in 1983, skeleton thin, with sunken eyes and hollowed-out cheeks, dying of starvation. She was my first conscious awareness of anorexia.) Once again, I shifted into super drive. I called and talked to local experts and I read books like *Reviving Ophelia: Saving the Selves of Adolescent Girls,* by Mary Pipher.

When Anne became ill that year, I decided to cut my practice hours back to seventy-five percent and job share with Jeff. This helped me spend more time with my daughter and take her to necessary appointments. I needed extra time with her and some breathing room for myself, but I was scared to death. I knew just enough about eating disorders to feel truly frightened about what was possible. And, getting her diagnosed and getting the help she needed took incredible effort.

Finding both a professional therapist and a nutritionist to work with Anne was reassuring. The nutritionist came highly recommended since she, sadly, took care of a lot of female athletes at the University of Texas at Austin. Fortunately, Anne liked her and agreed to work with her. It took about six months of "refeeding" to get our daughter back on track, gaining some weight, and feeling better. Just imagine how it might feel to observe your beautiful daughter measuring out the exact amount of peanut butter she planned to spread onto crackers and eat each day. She counted out strawberries and apple slices, cups of milk and cereal, and containers of yogurt. It was excruciating to watch that prescription for her—one that allowed her to control the smallest amounts of food she must eat.

It had been the perfect storm. Anne was the typical "at risk" teenager—intelligent, nervous, and perfectionistic. She had restrained emotions, compared to her siblings and her friends. She was affable and sociable, a real people-pleaser. Moreover, she had highly educated parents who had excessive expectations of all three of their children. Like other parents, we unwittingly put tremendous pressure on our bright children, who were heading toward good colleges. Eating disorders occur in five to thirteen percent of adolescent girls between the ages of thirteen and twenty. There is a unique combination of heredity, environment, culture, and conditioning that causes an eating disorder to develop. In today's culture, maintaining a positive body image and good self-esteem can be problematic for teenage girls, and because of this, dieting is more common than ever.

Eating disorders rarely resolve on their own. They also resolve more easily the sooner they are detected. If one daughter has an eating disorder, the entire family is affected. Anne's siblings can certainly attest to that. For at least a year, it seemed as if all we focused on was her eating. The teenager with an eating disorder always needs professional help. Even though we were willing to get professional therapy for ourselves, family involvement alone does not fix the eating disordered individual. Anne's case was typical, and I believe that her recovery was hastened by our early identification of the problem.

After her eating disorder was quiescent, Anne progressed along in high school enjoying her junior and senior years and swimming often. Then she noticed pain in her right hip. We feared it was a stress fracture from running, but hip X-rays were negative. Unexpectedly, an MRI showed a small tumor on one of her lower lumbar spinal nerves exactly where it exited the spinal canal. Phillip and I were terrified of what this might portend, but it turned out to be a Schwannoma, a benign tumor. These tumors most often pop up on the vestibular nerve, where they are called an acoustic neuroma. The Schwannoma is a rare tumor of the nerve sheath (the covering around the nerve). Anne underwent corrective neurosurgery at Children's Hospital, and her tumor was successfully resected from the nerve root without injuring the affected nerve. I gladly stayed with her in the PICU, where she lay flat on her back for three days. Her recovery went smoothly, and she had no loss of motor function to her right leg (what we feared might happen). Her friends rallied around her, visited often, and cheered on her recovery. Once again, my partners, Jeff and David, covered for me so that I could I stay home with her for the next two weeks until she returned to school. Competitive swimming was out, but she kept up her grades and continued to work toward graduation and starting college. In 2005, she happily began college at Southern Methodist University in Dallas.

As his high school years progressed, David enjoyed yearly scouting jamborees and special summer trips to New Mexico and Canada for long-distance hiking and canoeing experiences. He delighted in planning and cooking campout dinners for his patrol, and once was elected "iron chef" of his troop. Observing David growing up and finding his solid footing in scouting granted me feelings of relief and satisfaction. David's ultimate scouting experience was, of course, Philmont Scout Ranch, Boy Scout heaven—a high adventure base camp located in the mountains of New Mexico. He was chosen as crew leader and as such had to supervise seven other boys. He had two adult helpers on that expedition. One of the fathers, my own cardiologist, served as his adult helper and told me much later that David had been key in convincing his own son to stay the course when he wanted to call it quits early on. Hearing that story was reassuring and extremely gratifying. At Philmont, the groups trekked for two weeks, making their way through the mountains, reading maps, finding, or making shelters, treating unclean water, cooking, and feeding themselves.

We were thrilled when David advanced to Eagle Scout, as many of the Troop 990 boys did. He deserved this distinction since he had worked diligently to learn so many new and exciting skills. (My older brother, Ted, was an Eagle Scout, and he made sure that I was aware of the significance of this achievement.) With great pride, we arranged a huge dinner celebration for David and his troop after his Eagle Scout Court of Honor, which was attended by both his uncle Ted and his granddaddy. Instead of formal decorations, I hung every one of his boy scout T-shirts, at least twenty, around the fellowship hall at our church. All his troopmates, scout leaders, and our friends and family attended, and we enjoyed a buffet of tacos el carbon with all the fixings. I have never been prouder.

David continued to play bass in the orchestra throughout the rest of middle school, all high school, and all his college years. During his senior year in high school, he was elected Orchestra President, an unexpected accomplishment. This group of teens were called "orc dorks," since all of them were bright, nerdy, and musical. He fit into that group perfectly, and David seemed content throughout high school. I gladly watched my husband become the official orchestra parent chaperone. When the high school orchestra traveled around Texas, or to Breckenridge, Colorado, on yearly trips for competitions, Phillip would travel as their chaperone. He appreciated hanging out with Mr. Edmond, the congenial orchestra teacher, judging the students' cooking contests, and watching these interesting kids interact. Back at home, he delighted in telling me stories about their mischief.

During this time, my husband and I both enjoyed living in Austin, and we each appreciated the busyness and challenges of our separate practices. We each loved watching over our children as they grew and thrived. Each child seemed happy and active, although each had experienced hiccups along the way. I enjoyed working in the Seton NICU, sharing the load with my favorite partners, and caring for special, sometimes challenging, patients. My husband's practice was booming, and he recruited new subspecialty physicians to join them each year.

They quickly outgrew the Austin Children's Hospital and, in 2007, the new Dell Children's Medical Center slowly transformed from a great idea into a reality.

Chapter 13

A NEW PASSION

F or me, breastfeeding began as something healthy mothers could do for their babies. The medical benefits were substantial, so I naturally wanted to breastfeed my own children. But working full time and breastfeeding is problematic, to say the least, and there are many barriers to overcome along the way. Returning to work soon after the birth of my first child and using a hand-held, battery-operated breast pump was a recipe for failure. At the time, I didn't understand the feed-back cycle of demand and supply. I got busy in the NICU, didn't sit down often enough to pump, and, as a result, my milk supply dwindled. With my second child, I returned to work again at eight weeks but used an electric, hospital-grade breast pump. My adequate milk supply lasted several months longer until the stresses of busy NICU workdays took a toll and I carved out insufficient time for pumping.

From the beginning of nursing Anne, I had tremendous trouble with engorgement and sore nipples. She nursed like a shark, and my nipples were raw, cracked, and painful for three weeks. Sometimes they bled. I also struggled through a horrible bout of mastitis when she was six weeks old. Somehow, we made it over that high hurdle of sore nipples, and everything healed. My pediatrician brain didn't remember to put my finger into her mouth and assess her suck, and my mother brain never considered it. Much later, I figured out that she probably had ankyloglossia, or tongue-tie. How could I have missed that? (In ankyloglossia, the frenulum, or anchoring tissue under the tongue, is so tight or thick that it prevents the tongue from extending properly. A tongue thus tethered to the bottom of the mouth creates an abnormal and harmful suck.)

Visiting with the preemie moms while pumping in the quiet, comfortable pumping room adjacent to the NICU at TCH was pleasant. The walls were adorned with posters of angelic young moms, snuggled comfortably in rocking chairs, gazing lovingly at their nursing preemies. The atmosphere was serene and soothing as we sat in soft recliners listening to our pumps whirring and pulsating. It was fun to hear their stories, and I interjected encouragements for them along the way. When I was a young mother in the mid-1980s, breastfeeding was coming back in style. La Leche League was encouraging all mothers to breastfeed. (Their book, *The Womanly Art of Breastfeeding*, was first published in 1991.) My preemie moms had even greater incentive to express their milk because of all the medical benefits of breastmilk feedings for premature infants that were identified.

While nursing Anne, I was working with a bright and spirited self-starter pediatric resident. After telling him my own two trying breastfeeding stories, and helping the moms in our unit, he decided to write a paper about the practical aspects of breastfeeding. We wrote that paper together, and it was quickly accepted for publication.[5] That resident is today a well-respected, academic, pediatric department chairman in the Midwest with countless publications in his curriculum vitae. The process of interacting with residents and guiding them in clinical research or publications can be rewarding, not only for the trainee, but also for the faculty member. In that one experience, breastfeeding became not just personal, but an area of clinical interest and expertise.

When we moved to Little Rock in 1991, I was nursing my third child. Laura was an easy baby, a pleasure to nurse for twelve months. I returned to work when she was four months old and continued nursing and pumping my breastmilk

---

5   A practical guide to successful breast-feeding management. Freed GL, Landers S, Schanler RJ. *Am J Dis Child.* 1991 Aug; 145(8):917-21.

for another eight months. This enabled our nanny to feed her breastmilk when I was working. Finally, breastfeeding was a nice experience. Only once did we have any sort of mishap. At eight months of age, while cuddled together in a rocker nursing, she bit me—hard, on the nipple—and I screamed at her, "No biting!" She burst into tears, and we both cried and cried; after that, though, I experienced no more biting.

Opening the NICU Milk Bank at Arkansas Children's Hospital allowed me to feel as if I had some real expertise in breastfeeding and milk banking, mostly based on my personal and bedside clinical experience. I partnered with a pediatric gastroenterologist at UAMS and together we took breastfeeding courses and conducted seminars locally. We traveled to San Diego, to "WellStart International," a preeminent breastfeeding research center for training. At that time there were very few educational curricula for breastfeeding, and none were offered by the American Academy of Pediatrics.

When we relocated to Texas in 1997, my friend, the gastroenterologist, told her colleagues at the Texas Department of Health and Human Services, or DHHS, that I was a breastfeeding "expert." Previously, while she was on faculty at University of Texas at San Antonio, she conducted educational seminars on breastfeeding for DHHS. So, the staff at Texas DHHS hired me to travel around the state and provide similar educational seminars for physicians and nurse practitioners. At that time, it was well known that physicians were not adequately trained in the science of breastfeeding. Furthermore, they had been heavily influenced by the educational offerings provided by formula companies during residency. That made it easy for them to reach for formula when they encountered mothers and babies with breastfeeding problems in their practice. The DHHS seminars fulfilled a statewide need, were well received, and allowed me to do something that felt academic.

I traveled to twelve Texas cities, meeting other physicians and teaching. Front-line physicians around Texas—family practitioners, pediatricians, and obstetricians—were trying to do the right thing and support breastfeeding mothers. I was able to interact with a nice combination of men and women who were eager to learn. None of them expressed prejudicial pro-formula attitudes. However, none had been trained adequately to support breastfeeding.

The physicians and NPs who attended the DHHS seminars wanted to learn proper techniques and clinical practices to support breastfeeding moms and were awarded free CME credits for their time. Each was eager to support the type of feeding that seventy-five percent of new mothers in Texas chose. Participating in the Texas Breastfeeding Coalition put me in contact with other professionals, such as LCs and public health officials, interested in promoting breastfeeding around the state. I valued these activities, except that each was performed during my personal time off from clinical practice.

Moving to Austin and joining a private practice group heightened my desire to pursue a new area of professional expertise, to pursue a new passion. Continuing to teach breastfeeding management around the state and writing an educational offering for Pediatrix Medical Group (now Mednax), my employer, was just the beginning. I began to collaborate with other pediatricians and obstetricians who cared about breastfeeding and joined the Academy of Breastfeeding Medicine, or ABM. This was an international group of physicians who believed there was a need for additional training for physicians in the science of breastfeeding medicine. Much of the work done in the early years of ABM consisted of producing policy statements and clinical guidelines to counteract the influence of formula companies.

In 2002, I was chosen as one of the first sixteen fellows of the ABM. FABM was a distinction that required a rigorous application and selection process. Documentation of hours of teaching, clinical service, and/or clinical research in breastfeeding, publications,[6] and letters of recommendation were required. When chosen, I was ecstatic and felt honored to be among a group of some renowned names in breastfeeding. With me in that first group of FABMs was Dr. Ruth Lawrence, who had written the first book specifically for doctors, *Breastfeeding: A Guide for the Medical Profession*, originally published in 1980, and now in its eighth edition. Ruth is considered one of the grandmothers of breastfeeding medicine. However, it was disappointing that the distinction FABM did not mean much back home in private practice. After nearly twenty

---

6   Maximizing the benefits of human milk feeding for the preterm infant. Landers S. *Pediatr Ann.* 2003 May; 32(5): 298-306. Review.

years of practicing neonatology, I found myself still caring about what others thought of my credentials and my expertise.

Around the same time, the Mother's Milk Bank at Austin was growing in prominence. This was different—a milk bank devoted solely to storage and processing of donor breastmilk to be used for preterm babies all over the state. Healthy mothers, nursing healthy babies, who had been screened prenatally and were negative for HIV, Hep B, and Hep C, gladly donated their milk. They brought in hundreds of bottles and bags of milk, mostly white, some creamy-yellow, and others grayish. I voluntarily served as medical director of the Mother's Milk Bank at Austin from 2000 to 2004. This role was fascinating since initially I knew little about donor milk banking. I fielded many questions from donor moms about the medications they took, and whether those meds prohibited their donating milk. On several occasions we were able to help a bereaved mother gather up her previously expressed breastmilk and donate it to the Austin Mother's Milk Bank. If a mom had a lot of breast milk in storage after her baby died, she was comforted by the idea of donating her milk so that other preemies might use it.

The donor breastmilk was stored in a huge, stainless steel walk-in deep freeze, one with alarms for deviant temperatures. The date of collection, date of donation, and date of thawing were all carefully noted. Donated breastmilk was thawed, then pooled, usually five or six mothers' samples added together, and pasteurized so that no bacteria or viruses could be transmitted to the infant. Donor milk must be sterile before it is refrozen and dispensed to NICUs. Hospitals paid between $2.50 and $4.00 per ounce for the pasteurized milk and maintained certain quantities frozen locally to use for their babies when mothers could not, or would not, pump their own.

In 2002, Pediatrix Medical Group donated a MilkoScan so that nutritional analyses could be performed, and the donor milk was labeled with the content of protein, carbohydrate, fat, and calories. Higher caloric density donor milk was created for the tiniest preemies. Mothers who could not breastfeed often consented to use donor breastmilk for their preterm infants in hopes of gaining benefits for their own babies. Although mother's own breastmilk is the best food and protection for premature babies, donor breastmilk is next best compared to preterm formula. Both mothers' own and donor breast milk are fortified to ensure proper nutrition and growth. (A recently published meta-analysis demonstrated that feeding preterm infants with artificial formula—rather than donor breast milk when mother's own breast milk is not available—is associated with faster rates of growth, but with a near-doubling of the risk of developing necrotizing enterocolitis, or NEC.[7]

Later on, I served as a member of the milk bank's Board of Directors from 2005 to 2009. That experience was tedious, and involved reviewing budgets, grants, fund-raising, and personnel issues. In 2010 we published a paper about bacteria in donor milk before and after pasteurization using some of our local data.[8] Donor human milk banking in the U.S. exploded between 2000 and 2016. When the Mother's Milk Bank at Austin opened in 1998, there were only eight donor milk banks around the country. Now there are twenty-nine members of the Human Milk Bank Association of North America.

Dr. Richard Schanler, a neonatologist colleague and friend from Baylor, who conducted research in human milk, invited me to join a new Section on Breastfeeding within the American Academy of Pediatrics, or AAP. Six pediatric pioneers in breastfeeding medicine created this new section and authored the first policy statement for general pediatricians on "Breastfeeding and the use of human milk," published in 1997. As a member of the section, I was privileged to participate in subsequent revisions of that same policy statement, republished in 2005 and 2012.[9] Attending section meetings at the AAP annual conference was not only stimulating but also delightful since meetings were held in large cities around the U.S., and the AAP covered travel expenses. Making new friends and networking with other breastfeeding "experts" from Nashville, Denver, Seattle, San Diego, Palo Alto, Orlando, Pittsburgh, Cincinnati, and Rochester, was a thrill. The section's educational

---

7   Quigley M, Embleton ND, McGuire W. Formula versus donor breast milk for feeding preterm or low birth weight infants. *Cochrane Review.* July 2019. https://www.cochrane.org/CD002971/NEONATAL_formula-versus-donor-breast-milk-feeding-preterm-or-low-birth-weight-infants

8   Bacteriological screening of donor human milk before and after Holder pasteurization. Landers S, Updegrove K. *Breastfeed Med.* 2010 Jun; 5(3):117-21.

9   Breastfeeding and the use of human milk. Section on Breastfeeding. *Pediatr.* 2012 Mar; 129(3): e827-1. Epub 2012 Feb 27.

programs quickly increased in popularity as more pediatricians signed on to learn how to clinically support breastfeeding. At the time, seventy-five percent of new mothers were choosing to breastfeed, and pediatricians figured they needed to learn how to help them.

At home, I provided free breastfeeding in-services to L&D, NICU, and newborn nursery personnel throughout our Seton hospital network in all six hospitals where babies were delivered, and I presented more grand rounds. We began to make weekly breastfeeding rounds in the NICUs. Mostly, our bright and caring NICU nurses needed a champion for their cause, and I gladly stepped into that role. I liked talking to breastfeeding moms and agreed to help whenever a problem popped up with a mom or baby among my partners' patients. I also relished the distinction as a regional breastfeeding expert.

Many NICU moms struggled with mastitis but kept it secret from us. A lot of them developed yeast infections, which required treatment of both mother and baby to eradicate. I enjoyed seeing these moms; it seldom felt like extra work. All our NICU personnel—the nurses, LCs, educators—worked toward common goals of helping more NICU mothers express their milk, increasing rates of human milk feedings, and improving breastfeeding (actual nursing) among our NICU babies. My partners were supportive, but not as hands-on as I was.

There was one unforgettable, startling case. Little Jeremy was a small, near-term baby born six days earlier weighing six pounds. He went home breastfeeding and saw his private pediatrician on day six after birth, when he weighed only five pounds. The pediatrician could not believe that he lost one pound since birth, was appropriately concerned about his jaundice, and sent the baby from his office to our NICU. We found his birth record, reweighed him and documented that, truly, he had lost one whole pound in a week. The turgor of the jaundiced skin over his chest and abdomen was so dry that it "tented" upon gentle pinching. He was profoundly dehydrated with a dangerously high bilirubin level of 20 mg/dl, a low serum glucose (blood sugar) of 40 mg/dl, and a high serum sodium of 153 mEq/l. On admission he was quite simply starving.

Fortunately, his extreme dehydration responded to IV fluids, and intensive phototherapy lowered his bilirubin. The baby was fed some formula and a little of mother's expressed breastmilk. However, Jeremy's young mom was devastated since her milk had not "come in" yet. She looked exhausted, weak, and was often tearful. Her very sleepy baby had not demanded feedings often enough to stimulate her milk supply, and being a first-time mother, she didn't understand how breastfeeding works. In addition, she allowed him to suck on a pacifier frequently. The more often a baby nurses, the more stimulation there is for milk production and the better mother's milk supply. A baby sucking on a pacifier is not sucking on his mother's nipple.

The LC worked with his mother to increase her milk supply, and Jeremy fed voraciously and gained weight quickly. Mom remained wary, but we provided a lot of cheerleading and encouragement to keep her nursing. This kind of breastfeeding "disaster" was being reported around the country at that time. Poorly breastfed babies were getting into serious trouble within the first week of life. As a result of cases much like Jeremy, the AAP changed its recommendation from the traditional two-week follow-up visit after birth to a newly revised guideline recommending that full-term breastfed babies be seen within three to five days after hospital discharge.

Our NICU breastfeeding support programs created comfortable pumping rooms for the moms, although some preferred to pump at the bedside. They pulled up a rocker and footstool, gazed at their baby while hooked up to an electric breast pump, and produced more milk as a result. The mothers who held their baby skin to skin, not wrapped in a blanket, had even greater milk output. We encouraged skin-to-skin holding for all the babies, so called "kangaroo care," which was first described in the 1970s as a life-saving measure undertaken in South American hospitals where incubators were either unavailable or unreliable. There, mothers kept their own preterm baby inside their shirts, snuggled against their breasts. Studies showed that kangaroo care provided not only warmth and nutrition to premature babies who would otherwise succumb, but also prevented hospital-acquired infections. Years later, U.S. data confirmed that skin-to-skin holding stimulated maternal breastmilk production, probably mediated through the increased secretion of the hormone oxytocin (sometimes called the bonding hormone). Such a sensible notion—that a mother cuddling her baby on her chest made more milk.

We knew that mothers of the smallest preterm babies had the most trouble maintaining their milk supply while pumping over many weeks, so we had willing moms practice skin-to-skin care with their baby at least daily. Imagine a tiny preemie, say 800 grams, hooked up to a ventilator, with a central venous line and feeding tube dangling from his scrawny body, electrodes pasted to his chest and leg, wearing only a miniature diaper, being lifted off of his warmer and placed gently onto mom's chest. A warm blanket was then placed over him and his mother's chest. The NICU nurses and respiratory therapists made coordinated, patient efforts to ensure that this snuggling, bonding time happened without incident. Afterwards, many moms noticed an increased milk supply. Talking with the NICU moms and nurses about the science behind breastfeeding and human milk production felt satisfying.

One young mother of twin baby girls remains prominent in my memory. She was an engaging schoolteacher, happy to have twins, who stayed at her babies' bedsides daily. She sat and read to them, and dutifully pumped her milk often. Her twins were large preemies, born at 30 weeks gestation. They had minimal respiratory distress and mild apnea, or breathing pauses, and were normally feeding and growing when, at one month of age, one of the girls acted puny and exhibited worse apnea. Concerned about infection, possible sepsis, we began IV antibiotics. The baby girl recovered nicely, but, surprisingly, her blood culture grew group B Strep, that vicious microbe that in past years killed so many babies. I was baffled about the source of this organism in a one-month-old, until their mother confided that she had been struggling with mastitis (a breast tissue infection) for over a week. Her doctor had prescribed an antibiotic to which she did not respond. This mom's left breast remained bright red, swollen, and tender, and that day she was in tears.

Cultures of the mom's breast milk grew Group B Strep. This organism had been reported to cause mastitis, but only rarely. Upon hearing the news, this fragile, new mother was distraught. I explained that many mothers pass bacteria along in their breastmilk during mastitis, reiterating that this was a totally treatable infection—for her and her babies—but that did little to assuage her. By then she felt embarrassed and anxious, and confided that she felt guilty and needed assurance that she could not "hurt" her girls again. In her mind, the only way to do this was to stop breastfeeding. Accepting this mom's decision made me sad, but, of course, I understood her feelings of guilt and disappointment.

In 2010, Pediatrix Medical Group, conducted an internal audit of all its NICUs around the country, more than five hundred at that time, and discovered that our NICU at Seton Medical Center was among those few with the highest rates of human milk use and highest prevalence of babies going home partially breastfeeding. At that time, human milk feedings were well known to prevent necrotizing enterocolitis, or NEC, a serious bowel infection, and to lower the risk of hospital-acquired sepsis, or bloodstream infections. Soon thereafter, data from the NICHD Neonatal Network showed that human milk feedings were associated with improved neurodevelopmental outcomes for extremely low birth weight babies followed until twenty-four months of age. Pediatrix took what we were doing in our NICU, delineated our practices, and shared it with all their other NICUs. (In retrospect, this was another missed opportunity for a publication.)

The AAP continued to train general pediatricians in breastfeeding management. Being invited to speak at national meetings about breastfeeding support in the NICU, managing breastfeeding problems after hospital discharge, and NICU milk banking was gratifying. I was invited to co-author a paper about donor milk banking for *Pediatric Clinics*.[10] Ultimately, I was elected to the Executive Committee of the Section on Breastfeeding. This was not a paid position; however, the AAP did reimburse my travel expenses. I happily served in that capacity for six years, from 2008 to 2014, and used my personal time off from clinical duties to attend these meetings. Unfortunately, my practice didn't provide coverage for these trips.

In 2012 the Section on Breastfeeding published its revised policy statement "Breastfeeding and the Use of Human Milk" for pediatricians. We were proud when it became the most frequently downloaded policy statement authored by the AAP that year. In 2012, our team of breastfeeding support staff (nurses, dieticians, LCs) presented an award-winning abstract at the AAP national meeting, describing the "Prevalence of Patients Discharged Home on Breast Milk

---

10   Donor human milk banking and the emergence of milk sharing. Landers S, Hartmann BT. *Pediatr Clin North Am.* 2013 Feb; 60(1): 247-60. Review.

Feedings in Three NICUs." Our rates were well above the sixty-sixth percentile nationally for the whole company. My last scholarly endeavor for the AAP was to co-author a policy statement entitled "Donor Human Milk for the High-Risk Infant," which was published in 2017,[11] after I retired.

Pursuing a new area of professional proficiency—breastfeeding management and donor human milk banking—provided an avenue for maintaining academic excellence throughout the latter half of my career. Breastfeeding medicine became not only my expertise, but also my passion, and allowed me to contribute my knowledge of NICU breastfeeding support to local and national efforts. Currently there are hundreds of pediatricians, neonatologists, and obstetricians around the country who are skilled in breastfeeding management, most of them members of ABM or the Section on Breastfeeding in the AAP. These physicians carry the torch for breastfeeding advocacy, support, and training. Moreover, many general pediatricians avail themselves of the AAP's educational offerings about breastfeeding support at national annual meetings. We made tremendous progress.

---

11 Donor Human Milk for the High-Risk Infant: Preparation, Safety, and Usage Options in the United States. Committee on Nutrition; Section on Breastfeeding; Committee on Fetus and Newborn. *Pediatr. 2017 Jan; 139(1)*

Chapter 14

COMPLICATIONS

Every so often in the practice of medicine, complications arise even when a procedure seems to go well. Early in my career, one case at TCH stood out: a newborn with a depressed skull fracture. He was born by forceps-assisted vaginal delivery by a talented obstetrician. Talking with the parents and the labor nurse reassured me that the stainless-steel forceps blades had been placed properly around the baby's head and used correctly to gently guide his delivery. No torsion was exerted, and no unnecessary pulling was described. Soon after birth, however, the baby had a brief seizure that prompted his admittance to the NICU. There was a peculiar spot at the top of his forehead on the left where his skull was dented in like a ping-pong ball. His neurological exam was normal, but a CT scan of his head revealed the depressed skull fracture and a grape-sized epidural hematoma. This is a hemorrhage, or blood clot, that lies underneath the skull bone and presses on top of the brain. The hematoma required surgical evacuation, and the depressed fracture needed lifting. After undergoing neurosurgery that day, the baby returned to the NICU very stable. He recovered nicely and his coagulation, clotting, studies proved to be normal. The parents were told that this was "just one of those things—sometimes complications happen." This obstetrician knew these parents well and, as a result, they coped nicely with the occurrence and never threatened litigation. Fortunately, their baby recovered fully.

Years later, a similar case at Seton Medical Center did not conclude so happily. An obstetrician delivered a nine-pound baby boy whose heart rate was down during the final stage of delivery. There were no other signs of fetal distress. This doctor used a vacuum extractor (instead of forceps) to assist the vaginal delivery. He felt competent in using this device, just as he had done many times before. This time, however, he must have been impatient. Later, the L&D nurses reported that he tried forceps initially, then switched to the vacuum extractor. (Using more than one device is generally more hazardous.) The nurses remembered that he applied some torsion when pulling on the vacuum, and after three "pop-offs" (the vacuum cup actually pops off the scalp), he continued tugging on the vacuum until the baby was delivered. At birth, the baby's scalp was notably bruised and slightly swollen, and he needed mild stimulation and blow-by oxygen after delivery. Then his head began to swell.

Within a period of two hours, his scalp lifted off his skull from his eyebrows down to the base of his neck and extended behind both ears. This was a huge subgaleal hemorrhage (a blood collection above the skull periosteum, the covering over the bone, and below the scalp fibrous tissue). It carries a high mortality rate. The blood accumulation under the scalp steals blood from the rest of the body and causes shock. The large, boggy blood clot under the scalp leads to a coagulation disturbance called disseminated intravascular coagulation, or DIC. In the NICU, this baby required countless blood and plasma transfusions, platelet transfusions, and several medications to treat his shock and DIC. Tragically, this baby died, but his death prompted a hospital-wide quality review of assisted vaginal deliveries, those performed by forceps or vacuum extraction. His death also generated a routine perinatal death review by obstetrical colleagues, and as such, the results remained protected as peer-reviewed, privileged medical staff material.

Several obstetricians and L&D nurses volunteered to participate in the hospital's quality improvement, or QI, effort. The hospital risk-management department provided us with a perinatal data manager, a person to crunch the numbers. I volunteered as the neonatologist for this project—my motivation being a personal bias against the use of vacuum extractors. Our team reviewed several years of maternal and infants' charts and operative notes for all assisted vaginal deliveries, and we found a common use of the vacuum extractor. Some OBs felt comfortable with the vacuum and others preferred forceps; their preference usually resulted from their residency training. Our review highlighted a number of instances of paralysis of the facial nerve, other smaller, less severe subgaleal hematomas, two cases of subdural hematoma (a blood clot outside of the brain, below the dura, the outermost layer covering the brain), two skull fractures, numerous cephalohematomas (a localized collection of blood just above the bone but localized within the scalp), and a lot of scalp abrasions and bruising. All these conditions taken together are called birth trauma. Pediatricians and neonatologists who had noticed and cared for these newborn complications generally assumed they were just the unlucky, high price that babies paid for a traumatic or difficult delivery.

Next, our team reviewed the current clinical guidelines for use of forceps and vacuum extractors recently updated and published by the American College of Obstetricians, or ACOG. We developed a clinical checklist for all assisted vaginal deliveries and granted permission for nurses to question obstetricians about the procedure in real time, during the actual delivery. Most interestingly, we reported each prior instance of birth trauma to each delivering OB, and anonymously to all the OB medical staff. Most were surprised that such a high rate of complications had occurred, and all agreed that published evidence-based clinical guidelines should be followed. Initially, none of the OBs appreciated L&D nurses asking questions, and certainly none wanted to be questioned about outcomes, but later they grew accustomed to it. We met monthly to review data and adherence to previously agreed upon clinical protocols for use of vacuum and forceps. Over the course of a year, our new process lowered our institutional rate of birth trauma significantly, and we all felt proud for accomplishing something important. The second year produced even better results.

Several team members wrote and published a peer-reviewed paper,[12] and our data and QI process were presented at QI meetings around the country. Some of the L&D nurses were lauded with considerable notoriety for their work at these meetings, and their travel expenses were covered by the hospital's risk management department. Although this was not included in our publication, I like to recollect a comment made by one of the administrators from the risk management department, when, in one of our meetings, he opined to me, "The QI team efforts saved the hospital two million dollars in legal defense fees over the first two years of the initiative." No wonder the hospital administrators were happy to cover our expenses. Our "Road to Zero Preventable Birth Trauma" had been rough, but remarkable, and all the consequence of one baby's heartbreaking outcome.

Shortly after our publication in 2008, I was surprised to be awarded "Outstanding Accomplishment in CQI," from the Center for Research and Education of Pediatrix Medical Group. During this period, QI work continued to serve as a remedy to the grind of private practice. We worked with real-time clinical data, were empowered to gather teams of individuals to review data and make decisions and made use of published clinical guidelines as standards. David Brooks, in *The Second Mountain*, describes building collaborative teams by "using data as a flashlight, instead of as a hammer." We found this process to be surprisingly effective in changing behavior and encouraging practicing physicians to do the right thing. Without showing them actual data, most physicians do not believe there is a problem with their care.

A short time later, I was honored to be invited by an academic obstetrician from Seattle to co-author a paper on perinatal safety. Together we recounted our experiences with collaboration between neonatologists and obstetricians. We emphasized useful techniques and highlighted the importance of anonymous data sharing with practicing obstetricians. In 2010, our paper, "Perinatal Safety Programs and Improved Clinical Outcomes" was published in the *Clinics in*

---

12 The road to zero preventable birth injuries. Mazza F, Kitchens J, Akin M, Elliott B, Fowler D, Henry E, Landers S, Nix M, Ourston S, Sheppard C, Stallings D, Weihs D. *Jt Comm J Qual Patient Saf.* 2008 Apr;34(4):201-5.

Perinatology.[13] With my growing expertise in breastfeeding medicine, the recent award, and our efforts towards successful hospital-based QI work, I was feeling buoyant and reputable outside the realm of clinical NICU care. Twenty-five years into my career, it was fulfilling to still be contributing ideas and solutions. I was proud of my extracurricular pursuits and clearly imagined myself to be, at heart, an academic.

Nearly a year after our birth trauma initiative had run its course, we experienced an unusually severe case of respiratory distress syndrome, or RDS, that rocked the NICU. RDS is due to surfactant deficiency in premature babies. The affected baby boy's mother was the office nurse for a popular, local obstetrician. She was short, brunette, and fair. Her co-workers described her as reserved. This nurse-mother had a normal pregnancy but felt "fat and tired" in the last month, as so many of us do. She convinced her obstetrician (also her employer) to deliver her at 38 weeks gestation—full term is 40 weeks—by elective C-section for breech positioning. She wasn't in labor. The C-section went well, but her baby developed severe respiratory distress immediately after birth. Also, the infant appeared to be a large preterm baby, certainly not full-term. After transfer to the NICU, he required aggressive mechanical ventilation and artificial surfactant, a milky, fatty substance that coats the air sacs and allows them to stay inflated. Extra doses of surfactant provided minimal additional benefit.

During his first week in the NICU, this baby was so desperately ill and unstable that he almost qualified for extracorporeal membrane oxygenation—ECMO, or the heart-lung machine. Every day, his mother appeared dumbfounded as she stood quietly next to his bed beside the heaving ventilator and all the lines dripping fluids and medications into her newborn son. During the second week, he was only slightly better, so a lung biopsy was performed searching for a rare surfactant protein deficiency. That condition was ruled out, and finally, at three weeks of age, he began to improve. After five weeks of care in the NICU, he was well enough to go home. In retrospect, we all agreed that the baby had been born prematurely, around 35 or 36 weeks gestation, and suffered from lung immaturity and severe RDS. This little boy's life-threatening condition

---

13 Collaboration between obstetricians and neonatalogists: perinatal safety programs and improved clinical outcomes. Reisner DP, Landers S. *Clin Perinatol.* *2010 Mar;37(1):179-88. doi: 10.1016/j.clp.2010.01.009.*

occurred purely because of his elective C-section delivery. His mother's OB had presumed she was full-term, and without good obstetrical dates, he was wrong. Like so many other babies we cared for, he was an unexpectedly premature infant without adequate lung maturity.

After presenting this case as an unexpected-premature-baby-with-RDS to the OB section at a perinatal outcomes review session, several of the doctors were skeptical. When I opined that we often see cases of iatrogenic late prematurity and RDS in the NICU, they became angry. One well-respected OB, the leader of his practice group who had worked with us on the birth trauma initiative, said to me, "How dare you imply that we are creating prematurity." To which I replied, "You are not doing it on purpose, but, nevertheless, it's happening." Clearly, I sounded self-righteous and challenging that day, but my intent was to be brutally honest with them. I was weary of caring for late-preterm and early term babies who were delivered early, without medical indications, only to become sick with RDS. As expected, our obstetricians wanted proof of this phenomenon.

"Iatrogenic" means inadvertently caused by a physician, medical treatment, or diagnostic procedure. No obstetrician (and certainly no physician) wants to hear that he or she caused harm unduly. However, the previous decade had produced subtle changes in delivery patterns, locally and nationally. Mothers wanted a fixed delivery date so that their own OB could deliver them, and their OBs wanted to deliver Monday through Friday whenever possible. Elective deliveries by pitocin (oxytocin) induction increased, usually around 38 weeks gestation, and as a result, we in the NICU encountered more assisted vaginal deliveries and ultimately more C-sections. These trends were seen across the U.S., and neonatologists began to notice and discuss this surge in late preterm babies developing RDS.

I personally reviewed the previous two years' cases of RDS in larger preterm and near-term babies, born at 35–38 weeks gestation, at our institution. The data showed that each OB on staff delivered one, maybe two, cases per year of an unexpectedly premature infant who had RDS requiring NICU care. Altogether, there were 67 cases of RDS in our NICU among late preterm babies who had been electively delivered at our hospital during the previous two years. Given the large number of deliveries each year, over 8,000 at that time, no one individual OB noticed a problem. Nor did any of the obstetrical practices notice (a practice usually incorporating five or more OBs). Taken altogether, however, this was a significant amount of RDS in late preterm and near-term babies. The OB medical staff was impressed when I presented the actual numbers of babies who developed RDS, and I felt vindicated.

Our QI team convened again, with another obstetrician participating, and we reviewed ACOG clinical guidelines for elective induction and elective C-section delivery. The strongest indicators were 39 weeks gestation and active labor. Once again, we created clinical checklists for elective inductions, and we established the "39-week rule." OBs could no longer electively schedule a delivery prior to 39 weeks without a medical indication. This time the OBs acquiesced, and as a result, elective deliveries prior to 39 weeks gestation were not allowed simply for the convenience of the mother or her OB.

The Texas Department of State Health Services, based in Austin, heard about our efforts and invited some members of our team to present our data at a Texas Perinatal Association meeting. Our results were impressive, and shortly thereafter Texas Medicaid adopted the "39-week rule," and Medicaid refused to pay for any elective delivery before 39 weeks gestation. At the same time, all around the country other neonatologists were examining data and coming to the same conclusion—iatrogenic prematurity, or elective delivery before 39 weeks gestation, had become the biggest contributor to a surge in RDS among late preterm babies. The occurrence of one newborn's poor outcome prompted a significant change in local and statewide patterns of obstetrical care.

From my experience, I believe that when complications occur, data review is useful to elucidate the clinical issues at hand. Peer-reviewed, protected medical staff reviews do not necessarily change practices, however. Quality improvement teams that work collaboratively can identify outliers and suboptimal clinical practices. Provided that these teams include various subspecialties, and include bedside nurses, they can, with careful feedback to physicians, affect change and improve clinical practices. National physician organizations also have a significant role to play in updating clinical practice guidelines and educating physicians about them. I remain convinced that practicing physicians' participation in local, regional, and national organized medicine—and quality improvement initiatives—serves a higher purpose and is well worth the time and effort.

Throughout this stimulating period in my professional life, I was stressed at home by what our youngest child was going through. Unlike her sister, Laura headed toward high school with continued learning problems. Her ADHD seemed well controlled with medication, but she still needed tutors and accommodations to complete normal classes. It's embarrassing to admit that I helped her with geography and health, working through both of these online courses with her. She played violin in the orchestra but failed to practice and didn't care about it very much. She had enjoyed playing volleyball for several years in middle school. She was a strong middle blocker and went on to play for the junior varsity team in high school. But failing to make the varsity volleyball team was a crushing blow, and things went downhill for Laura.

By tenth grade, she was routinely written up for bad behavior and talking back in class. She began to skip school and got involved with an older boy from Fredericksburg, a nearby town. They met on a church mission trip in which he was supposed to be her "counselor." (To say that I regret having encouraged Laura to go on that church mission trip is a huge understatement.) She had several car wrecks in her green VW Beetle. The first involved carelessly plowing into the back of a car that was fully stopped. Her second happened at midnight while driving home from Fredericksburg—she fell asleep at the wheel and crashed into a tree. Luckily, she wasn't seriously injured. By her junior year, she was a horrid teenager, unbalanced and unchecked in every way. One afternoon, she purchased and brought home a pig from the pet store. She was thoroughly amused, but that day I lost it. I screamed at Laura and we had a huge fight. My husband stayed perpetually infuriated with her, yelled often, and attempted to keep us apart at home. It seemed as if we three were caught in a sick, codependent triangle of bad behavior.

Laura always had trouble with money, and the more we gave her, the more she spent. Sometimes she stole money from us. To our dismay, she got several tattoos, one on each inner wrist, and one on her hip. In Austin, tattoos are simple to come by, even though the age of consent is supposedly eighteen. I insisted that we visit her tattoo parlor together to see if they used sterilized equipment, and she rolled her eyes. One wrist tattoo spelled out FAITH, and the other HOPE. The tattoo on her hip was meant to show her hand in God's hand. I kept believing that she had a good character hidden deep down inside her. In addition to all her bad behavior and cries for help, she became alienated from her group of high school friends. Only Mr. Sanders, the mild-mannered, friendly, assistant principal, seemed to understand her troubles. He would listen to her excuses and merely assign her weekend detention or more community service hours. In our sessions with him and her math teacher, he would chuckle about her antics and reassure us that all this misbehavior was transient.

It is painful to describe just how unbelievably discouraged I felt about Laura during her high school years, and, in my heart, I felt like the wrong mother for her. She needed a patient, understanding, and compassionate mother, and I was nowhere close to that. In fact, some days I hated her. My three teenagers had presented me with a smorgasbord of events and challenges: Boy Scout treks, new swim teams, and varsity volleyball rejection. They had survived eating disorders, knife injuries, car wrecks, illegal tattoos, and nerve tumor resections. Each of their teenage challenges proved to be an incredible trial for me as well, and I no longer felt like the steadfast, loving, and supportive mother that I wanted to be.

Chapter 15

MULTIPLE BIRTHS AND
OTHER CHALLENGES

efore the recession began in 2008, Austin was booming. Our city was a technology hub and a lot of bright young minds had moved to the city to start new lives and create companies. Those tech workers, in addition to the large, highly educated faculty at the University of Texas at Austin, produced many couples who desired children, and many parents willing to use fertility drugs, such as Clomid, intrauterine insemination (IUI), and even in vitro fertilization (IVF) to have them. In an IUI procedure, doctors inject sperm into the uterus with a catheter. With IVF, doctors surgically retrieve eggs from the woman, fertilize them with sperm, and transfer the viable embryos back into the woman's uterus. Women can use their own or donor eggs. In 2007, IVF was extremely popular in Austin since insurance coverage for those services was offered to the employees of the large tech companies, such as Dell and Samsung. This issue was vital to us in the NICU because IVF pregnancies were far more likely to result in preterm births and multiple births. The risk of twins and triplets is vastly increased after IVF.

I listened to many parents' stories of their trials in navigating the limits of insurance coverage for themselves, their babies, and the financial surprises they encountered along the way. Health insurance coverage for maternity and infertility services was then, and is currently, a confusing web. Only forty-four percent of health plans cover IVF today. Parents suffering with infertility navigated through this chaos of health care coverage information. Only sixteen states now require infertility coverage by law. Although the number of companies that offer benefits for fertility treatment is on the rise, only four hundred companies in the U.S. offer these benefits. Even though some employers added infertility benefits, most IVF patients paid for all or some of their treatment out-of-pocket. A single round of IVF cost at least $20,000 in 2018. The average cost for one IVF cycle ranges from $12,000 to $15,000. These numbers don't include the cost of medications, which ranges from $1,500 to $3,000 per cycle.

In 2007, one of my obstetrician-friends and I partnered for a chart review of the timing of deliveries of multiple births. Our goal was to optimize NICU and L&D preparedness, another QI goal. Multiple births are mostly delivered by scheduled C-sections. The personnel and equipment necessary to care for multiples immediately after delivery is substantial, since most multiples are born prematurely, to varying degrees. The NICU crowd believed that these deliveries seemed to occur on Friday afternoons and throughout the weekend, when we were the least prepared and without extra personnel. The obstetricians felt that they were generally interspersed throughout the week. Our chart review confirmed the NICU prejudice, and thus, we began a dialogue to address the timing of these deliveries in the future.

So, imagine that you work in a busy NICU, routinely caring for sick and premature babies, mostly day in and day out, taking call in the hospital many nights and every other or every third weekend. This was our normal NICU set of affairs. Now imagine that within one calendar year, you cared for thirty sets of twins, eighteen sets of triplets, four sets of quadruplets, and one set of quintuplets. Those were the actual numbers from our 2007 review of multiple births.

That year, the quintuplets were delivered around 32 weeks gestation on a Sunday afternoon. I remember being called in from home to help. The babies were very stable, only three requiring ventilator support, so their care was relatively easy. The NNPs were inserting catheters and attending to IV fluids and medications while I volunteered to talk to the dad, go visit with mom, and get consent forms signed. I will never forget that young father looking up at me, shell-shocked. He was around thirty-five, tall and lanky, with short brown hair and a fair complexion. He looked like any other intelligent software engineer. After completing and signing his second set of papers, he looked up and asked, "Do I have to do this for each one?" He was serious. I almost laughed, but instead I just smiled and assured him that he now had five separate and distinct babies. And yes, there were separate forms to sign for each of his five children. These parents were blessed with wonderful support from their church. The church bought them a van, five car seats, five cribs, three strollers, and five highchairs. The couple graciously allowed the local newspaper to photograph their children and report their story. All five babies went home doing well and all were healthy when they returned for our Neonatal Reunion.

Two years later, another set of quintuplets graced our NICU. The parents of these babies started a television show to fund their medical costs and child-care needs. Their reality TV show began while they were in the NICU. Fortunately, all their babies had uneventful courses and struggled only with typical issues that premature babies face, like breathing and feeding. The parents allowed filming of their babies' care, and we talked to reporters and producers to answer any questions. After eight weeks in the NICU, all the babies were discharged home relatively healthy, and the show continued by following their home routine. "Quints by Surprise" was a big hit on the *Learning Channel* for about two years.[14] They also made two one-hour documentaries for TV. Those parents found such a creative way to pay their medical bills.

Because of their mother, Jessica, the Porter girls will forever remain my favorite set of triplets. Jessica and her husband had gone through IVF to conceive and birth these girls, and she treated each of them—and all of us—like a blessing. Alice, Franny, and Catherine were small babies, born at 26 weeks gestation,

---

14   "Quints by Surprise: Parents Say Show Creates Great Memories." *Austin American-Statesman*, Sept. 1, 2012.

weighing about 1,000 grams. Franny was the smallest, at 800 grams. Each girl struggled through the usual NICU challenges and therapies—lung immaturity, surfactant treatment and ventilator support, brain immaturity, breathing issues, intestinal immaturity, human milk feedings, and caffeine treatment (yes, caffeine: it helps as a respiratory stimulant). Their mother expressed her breastmilk for months, making enough to feed all three girls. Alice had an unusual cardiac arrhythmia (irregular heartbeat) that required medication. Franny developed a patent ductus arteriosus, or PDA, that required risky medication and weeks later corrective surgery (a PDA ligation). Then, Franny developed a bloodstream infection that was tricky to treat. Catherine just laid in her incubator acting perfect, feeding, and growing.

Their mother came in every day around 8 a.m. and sat with them all day long, happily reading and chatting with folks. She became a founding member of our NICU mothers' breastfeeding support group, which had recently been formed by our lactation consultant. She personally helped other moms who were struggling with their own milk supply. To me, she seemed to be a pillar of strength and poise. Her husband was often present as well, usually coming in after work to sit and read his *Wall Street Journal*.

Jessica remained composed and cheerful during her tenure in the NICU. She was a small young woman in her early thirties, with dark hair and clear brown eyes. She wore comfortable but stylish clothes. Of course, she looked worried from time to time, but I never once saw her cry. She was always there observing the routine NICU activity during her daughters' three-month stay. One day, she saw us resuscitate another baby in a nearby warming bed. She was nearby as we prepared for Franny's PDA ligation to be held right there in the NICU. She watched nervously as we cardioverted Alice the day she developed her unusual arrhythmia. Cardioversion is the procedure that sends electric shocks to the heart through electrodes placed on the chest to make its rhythm regular again—you've seen it, I'm sure, on medical TV shows. She witnessed us perform the procedure on her own tiny daughter. This young woman had an impressive positive attitude, and she was invariably composed. She recognized when the doctors were tired or sleepy after a long call night, and she was often amused by my excessive coffee intake on those mornings.

While her babies were in the NICU, she helped me personally by listening to my stories about my daughter Laura, and all her troubles in high school. In eleventh grade, when Laura began skipping school and smart-mouthing teachers, I became frustrated as a mother. After hours, when the NICU was quiet and all the work had been completed, we discussed Laura's crazy behavior. One morning, late into her daughters' care, all three girls were stable, and I needed to abruptly leave the unit. Laura had been missing for the previous two days. She drove over to Fredericksburg "to be with her boyfriend," and failed to return home at night. When Laura finally called, crying, "Mom, I want to come home," I was standing a few feet away from this mom. I burst into tears. Jessica listened briefly and said, "You need to go," so I excused myself and hurried out the door. Of course, I had a partner cover for me, but somehow this young mother gave me strength. For many years after her daughters went home, I relished receiving pictures and updates of the girls. Her three daughters are twelve years old now.

I read recently that Jessica organized an event in Austin that raised a large sum of money for an organization called Hand to Hold. This organization provides resources for NICU families. She shared her personal NICU journey and remembered that it took forty-two days before she held Franny for the first time. In retrospect, she wished that during those trying moments in the NICU "when she felt lost," that she would have accepted support and help offered by other parents, just the kind of support that Hand to Hold offers.

On a quiet Saturday evening in 2012, we were called STAT to the delivery of preterm twins at 30 weeks gestation. Luckily, there were two teams of personnel available for these potentially sick babies. Their febrile mother was in active labor and would be delivered vaginally. The first baby girl emerged headfirst, crying vigorously. She was dried, stimulated and turned pink quickly. With signs of minimal respiratory distress, our NNP carried her, wrapped in a blanket, over to see Mom and then the team whisked her off to the NICU. I waited for the second baby, who was advancing slowly. After an agonizing thirty minutes, she delivered, tightly folded into a V, with the middle of her back the presenting part. Her shoulders, head and arms were folded one way and her abdomen and legs were folded the other. In thirty years of attending high-risk deliveries, I had never witnessed a presentation like this.

I carried her to the resuscitation area in a warm blanket, dried, and quickly scanned her externally. She seemed about two pounds and had a huge, dark, bluish-purple bruise in the middle of her back, exactly where she had presented. We tried in vain to resuscitate her. Our efforts continued for thirty minutes, but there was no response in heart rate, and she never took a breath. I "called" the code (told my team when to stop our efforts) and brought the father in to see his baby. Dad was a young man in his thirties who looked drained and scared. I gently showed him his baby, especially the large bruise on her back, but I couldn't explain why she failed to respond to our resuscitative efforts. We both wondered out loud whether her back was broken, and I told the father, "that could be, but I have never seen that before." Then, the two of us took her to see her mother. He carried his dead infant in a blanket and placed her into his wife's arms. They cried together and he kissed her tenderly. Several hours later, I returned to sit with the parents, review everything that happened, and recommend to them that an autopsy would be helpful. Because we had no idea what caused her unusual and devastating delivery and death, they agreed to the post-mortem exam.

The delivering OB documented in the record, and told the parents, that she was an asynclitic delivery, which means she came out with her head tilted sideways toward her shoulder. This is not the same as a shoulder presentation, and not at all how she came out. Her reasons to record the presentation incorrectly were unclear to me. The next day I asked another OB why he thought his partner documented the wrong presentation in the medical record. Unbeknownst to me, earlier that day, a nurse had mentioned to him my concerns about a possible broken spine. He screamed at me, "How dare you suggest that my partner altered the record. I don't want you in my OR ever again." Although this OB was known to have a temper, his outburst was startling and not at all understandable. Providers were always edgy after an unexplained death, so he might have been preoccupied with that since the mother was his patient. Nevertheless, I had implied no such thing. I felt the baby's death was on me and wanted to understand what happened. Later, I reasoned that he must have felt that the baby's death was on his partner.

The infant's blood culture grew group B Streptococcus within one day, so that second twin obviously died of overwhelming infection. I sat quietly in mother's room and informed both parents of this. They were eager to hear an answer and were thankful for an explanation. The autopsy ruled out a broken spine and confirmed my physical findings denoting her extremely odd back-first presentation. The first OB never explained to me her incorrect documentation, but she was required to defend it to a perinatal death review committee. The second OB later apologized for screaming at me that morning.

Around that same period, there was another emergency delivery that made me so furious that I grimace whenever I recollect it. A young mother pregnant with twins at term was seen in her OB's office that morning. The doctor's nurse called L&D, then the NICU, to tell us that he planned to do an emergency C-section delivery. She reported that the babies were in trouble. Accordingly, the NICU staff prepared for two admissions, and two teams hurried down to L&D. When I arrived, the mother was sitting up in the OR having an epidural anesthetic inserted. I tiptoed in and whispered to the anesthesiologist, "Why aren't you using a general?" (General anesthesia is a much faster way to put mother to sleep.) He said he was told that there was time for an epidural. Sighing, I left to check on our team's preparations. Then, after ten more minutes, when the OB arrived, this mother's C-section began. We nervously anticipated a bad baby. The first twin boy came out crying and vigorous, but the second little boy came out blue, limp, and lifeless, with a heart rate around 50. Normal is 120 or greater.

I quickly took the baby into my warm blanket and hurried into the nearby stabilization area—only twenty feet away—where we began our efforts to resuscitate him. His heart rate barely responded to adequate ventilation. An endotracheal tube was inserted into his airway and secured. Meds were given via that tube with little response. Chest compressions were performed. A central venous catheter was quickly inserted into his umbilical cord, and meds were pushed directly into his little heart. By then, he had turned nice and pink, a sign of good oxygenation. Ten minutes after birth, he began to respond with a higher heart rate, but still he did not move or breathe. He began some gasping efforts around fifteen minutes of age, which was not a good sign. (The longer time it takes for a baby to begin gasping, the longer time he has been without oxygen and blood flow in utero.) At twenty minutes of age he was breathing regularly and stable enough to be transported to the NICU. The anesthesiologist popped in earlier while we were actively coding the baby to check on us, and he said, "Holy s***, now I know what you meant." With his remark, I gritted my teeth and clenched my jaw with anger but could do nothing more than keep working.

After we got him admitted to the NICU, I began to think about the communication between the OB, his nurse, the L&D staff, the anesthesiologist, and the NICU team. It had been appalling and confusing. Now we had this poor little boy who was severely distressed before delivery and displayed very low Apgar scores. He began to have seizures and developed hypoxic ischemic encephalopathy, or HIE—brain injury from low oxygen and low blood flow in utero. Later, there were more signs of neurologic damage. Two weeks passed, and he went home with an abnormal clinical exam and brain imaging evidence of significant brain damage.

Would a C-section ten or twenty minutes sooner have made a difference? I think so, but couldn't be sure, however, I never said so. These parents were in their thirties, both quiet and restrained. They asked few questions of my partner, who cared for their son. Certainly, they were overwhelmed with one baby downstairs in the nursery and one in the NICU. The couple always visited their son in the NICU together, and both seemed appropriately sad. Once I saw the mother's OB visiting the baby with them. My partner told me, "they just accepted what happened." Sometimes it is impossible to know how people process bad news and which details they recall and attempt to piece together. Maybe the mother felt guilty. Maybe the OB satisfied them with a reason for the baby's poor outcome. I will never know, but we heard later that they never sued their OB.

Finally, a different kind of dramatic emergency remains unforgettable and exceptional. Only once in my career did I witness the result of giving a formula feeding directly into the lungs of a convalescing baby. This baby boy was six weeks old, had chronic lung disease, CLD, and a long and complicated course, but he was slowly improving. Babies with CLD generally take weeks to wean off the ventilator and even longer to wean out of oxygen. This little boy had a young, stressed-out, and angry mother. She always visited wearing jeans and T-shirts, had cropped black hair, and wore no makeup. She rarely smiled. Anyone could see that she was tired and irritated. She always visited her son alone and found fault with a lot of little things she observed the nurses doing. She complained that too many things had gone wrong with her infant's care (he had been born at 25 weeks gestation weighing 700 grams) and she was mad at everyone—the doctors, the nurses, her husband, everyone. Her baby had been born without exposure to antenatal steroids and developed severe RDS. Artificial surfactant had not proved beneficial. His patent ductus arteriosus, or PDA, had not responded to medical therapy and required surgical correction. This mom was active online and often blogged about her baby's care, all his problems, and her experience in the NICU. She had quite a following among other mothers, including the mothers of our other preterm infants. Everyone was worried about her anger and her blogging.

One fateful day, she was present in the NICU sitting at her son's bedside when a skilled nurse inserted a gastric feeding tube (usually a routine procedure) through his mouth and down into what she thought was his stomach. Somehow the tip of the tube ended up in his trachea, or main airway, instead. The nurse administered the formula feeding via that tube, and the baby immediately struggled, coughed, turned blue, and coded. The nurses asked the mother to leave the unit, but I insisted, "No, let her stay and watch." I was the doctor running the code. She sat in her rocking chair a few feet from all of us and observed as five or six of us resuscitated her baby and saved her small son's life. We gave medicines, we put in lines, we suctioned his airways, we took chest X-rays, and we checked blood gases. We sedated her thrashing son and finally our efforts paid off. He slowly began to improve and stabilize. She quietly sat there and watched everything that happened. (Babies with underlying lung disease are extremely demanding to resuscitate, as they have no pulmonary reserve.) It must have taken us two hours to get him completely stable. After that incident, her blog posts changed, and she never again wrote anything mean or angry about her experience in our NICU.

Emergencies bring out the best, or the worst, of health care providers and communication between them. Even though we train for emergencies, each one is different, and each provides a different lesson. Nowadays we conduct a debriefing after every resuscitation precisely so that we do not miss the lesson. When unexpected emergencies occur as the result of a procedural complication, like the feeding tube in the airway, we try to honestly explain what happened and why. Thankfully, we don't have to explain how much we care and how hard we work during a resuscitation.

One exceptional case, neither a multiple birth nor an emergency, must be shared. Dakota was a typical, fragile premature infant, and her mother, Emily, was a waif of a young woman, short, with mousy, straight brown hair and fair skin. In most respects, Emily resembled a typical young NICU mother, appropriately concerned and engaged. Her baby girl was born prematurely at 29 weeks gestation at Seton Medical Center. For many different reasons, her daughter had complications early in her NICU care and ended up with severe chronic lung disease. Dakota remained dependent on oxygen and mechanical ventilation at four months of age. The mother was a real trooper, however, always there for her baby, always informed about her care. She expressed her breast milk for months on end, which was fed to Dakota by tube, although the baby was never able to breastfeed. This mom happily visited and chatted with the nurses daily and always voiced her appreciation for their care. Sometimes Dakota developed pneumonia and other times she had bouts of sepsis. We were all astonished by the array of bacteria with which she became infected; so much so that we worked her up for an immune deficiency. The results were inconclusive.

At six months of age, still ventilator-dependent, Dakota was transferred from Seton to the NICU at Dell Children's Medical Center. Here she continued to have bloodstream infections, sometimes one immediately after another. By this time, she was an IV nightmare. That is, she had no reasonable IV access remaining and required a surgically inserted central venous catheter for antibiotic treatment. The nurses in her new NICU were not only frustrated but also perplexed by this baby. Emily remained pleasant and thankful, no matter how sick her infant became. An older, experienced NICU social worker suggested that we transfer the baby to the PICU for a night or two. There this mother and baby could stay together in a room while we videotaped them without the mother's knowledge. Emily and Dakota stayed there for two nights during which we recorded the mother wiping her baby's feces onto her central line access point, twice. We captured the mother on a surveillance camera contaminating her own daughter's central line, in an effort to start another infection.

Dakota was removed from her mother by Child Protective Services and the court.[15] Her mother was convicted of a first-degree felony and sentenced to twenty years in jail.[16] This condition is called Munchausen syndrome by proxy, and it's a form of child abuse. The mentally ill parent sabotages the child's care in order to continue to receive attention. Experts do not know what causes it but think it may be linked to problems during the abuser's childhood, perhaps emotional trauma or illness resulting in extensive medical attention. The caregiver, usually a mother, shows patterns of abnormal thinking and behavior, as they feign illness or symptoms to make their child look ill. The attention that the abuser parent gets from having a sick child encourages their behavior.

This mother was typical in that she seemed devoted to her child and she tried to become close and friendly with the nursing staff. Although her abnormal behavior represented her need to feel powerful or in control, Emily didn't see her own behavior as harmful. Dakota's case was truly astonishing and the only case of Munchausen syndrome by proxy that I personally experienced during my long career. The hallmark is an abuser parent seeking praise from others for their devotion to their sick child. However, no mother in her right mind would choose to harm her baby merely for attention. Only a mentally deranged mother could do this.

---

15 *Austin American Statesman*, "Mother accused of injuring child with feces returns to jail." June 4, 2009.

16 "Mom smeared feces on baby's IV tubing." April 5, 2011. www.statesman.com.

Chapter 16

THE TOUGHEST CLINICAL CASES

As neonatal intensive care patterns changed over the years and provided support to all babies, regardless of their chances of recovery, I began to witness more suffering. Thirty-five years of medical practice allowed me to watch countless babies and their parents struggle and suffer through severe illness. Some babies died quickly, and others lingered for days, even weeks. Their parents were usually with them in the NICU, going through it all. The longer I practiced, the more I thought that we provided treatments in the NICU that merely prolonged the dying process, instead of prolonging living. Or we offered treatments that ensured survival of a significantly damaged baby, one who would be profoundly disabled as a child or have an extremely poor quality of life. As the limits of viability declined as low as 22 to 23 weeks gestation, we offered treatment to babies whose parents hoped for a miracle, or who could not decide what to do and just wanted to try anything. For me, four special babies encountered in the last few years of my career best exemplify these complicated issues of neonatal intensive care, suffering, and dying.

Will was a tiny African American baby born at 27 weeks gestation, weighing 480 grams (less than one pound). His extremely low birth weight resulted from his mother's severe pregnancy-induced hypertension, or high blood pressure. He was a feisty little boy for several weeks and overcame his lung immaturity. His PDA was treated successfully with medication. But then he developed necrotizing enterocolitis; NEC is a serious bowel infection. He had many predisposing factors, but we all hoped that his being fed his mother's breastmilk would have prevented him from developing NEC. It is a serious, often deadly disease. His mom returned to work four weeks after his birth, then visited whenever she could. Will's father was a large man, a Baptist preacher who was extremely quiet and visited seldom. It was tough getting to know this mother since we talked mostly by phone. Occasionally she stopped by to visit him on her way home from her office. At these times she wore a stylish blue or gray work suit and conservative low heels, and her hair was nicely fixed in a short bob. I made a point of speaking to her in person whenever I could. At these times, however, she usually stood at his bedside, observing, and asking few questions. The nurses did not seem able to connect with her either.

When Will developed NEC around one month of age, he started going downhill. A bloodstream infection associated with his NEC spread to his lungs and he retreated to higher ventilator settings. His sepsis and NEC were treated with antibiotics and bowel rest (no feedings for two weeks). During this time, he was fed intravenously with hyperalimentation fluids. These fluids gave him protein, glucose, fats, minerals, and electrolytes, as well as all the vitamins he needed to grow. However, he grew poorly and slowly developed hepatitis, a complication of prolonged hyperalimentation. Then his liver started to fail. Many consultants saw him and offered suggestions for further evaluation and treatment, but none worked.

By three months of age he weighed only three pounds but reacted like a full-term baby; he was 39 weeks corrected age. He fussed often and cried real tears. Sometimes he flailed about in his pint-sized stainless-steel crib, decorated with mobiles, bull's-eye targets, checkerboards, mirrors, and pictures of his parents. He hated being stuck for labs; his little face always looked pained as he struggled against us. Keeping arterial lines in for lab monitoring and central lines for nutrition grew ever more laborious. His last central venous line caused a blood clot to develop proximal to the entrance to his heart. The obstructing clot caused his head and neck to swell with edema (fluid), and he began to resemble a black Casper the Friendly Ghost. The clot was treated with anticoagulants (blood thinners). I remember feeling both sad and discouraged upon giving his mother the news of this additional setback. Surely, she detected my sorrowful tone, but she reacted very little to this update, thanked me, and hung up.

By five months of age, it was clear that he was going nowhere slowly; he didn't tolerate re-feeding, and his liver failure worsened. My updates to his mother continued to be disappointing, since her son made little progress. Finally, one day at his bedside, I broached the subject of comfort care, but his mother looked down, frowning, and shook her head. She said she "didn't want to talk about that." Even though she began to visit more often, she rarely held him. However, Will's father started to visit again. These parents were obviously hurting and desperately trying to do the right thing, but they wouldn't open up or talk to any of us.

It was not until Will was six months old that we convinced his parents to provide comfort care and no further increase in support. A sit-down care conference was convened and included his primary nurses, two neonatologists, the social worker, and chaplain. That day, when everyone agreed that further therapy for his condition was futile, his parents finally agreed to comfort care. However, they were not prepared to withdraw him from the ventilator. After our conference, his mother came in daily and held him for long periods while she rocked him. She was saying goodbye finally, but his father stopped visiting again. Will died two weeks later, resting comfortably in his mother's arms. Will's mother was stoic and had no tears that day. She didn't seem to believe me when I told her how sorry I was. The afternoon he died, she looked up at me and thanked me for all we had done for her son.

Will's case bothered me for a long time. I think that we all kept him too long, that we put him through too much. I believe that this little boy truly suffered throughout the last few months of his short life. He often looked up at us as if he did not understand why we kept hurting him. Despite sedatives and swaddling, holding, cooing, and rocking by the nurses, and sometimes by me, all he ever knew was a life of light and noise and pain in the NICU.

Around the time that Will was being cared for through all his months of struggles, I would come home and murmur to my husband, "I wish that poor baby would die." We talked about our most troublesome patients at the dinner table with our children present. They grew up listening to our stories and visiting the hospitals and the NICU where I worked. In past years, the older two frequently made rounds with their father on weekends. They talked to nurses and sometimes met patients and their parents. Occasionally they walked around inside the NICU with me when the unit was quiet at night. I remember Anne commented on the babies' little hands and feet and how much they liked to suck on miniature pacifiers. David observed that the smallest preemies looked like hot dogs between buns wrapped in Saran Wrap under a warming lamp. Indeed, we did use Saran Wrap blankets to cover the smallest babies to prevent excessive fluid losses through their skin.

One evening at supper when Laura was fourteen, she asked me a tough question. At that time, she was typically testy and blurted out, "Why do you want to be a doctor and care for babies if you want them to die?" Her comment startled me, and I wondered how often she had heard me say something like this to my husband. I explained that only some of the sickest babies needed to die, in fact, very few of them. I explained that most of my patients recovered, grew, and thrived. Not only did I make up my mind to be more careful about what I said at the dinner table, but also, I took Laura to the NICU one Saturday night soon after when the unit was quiet.

We walked around to see every baby, mentioning him or her by name. If the parents were there, I introduced Laura to them. I told her a little bit about each baby and picked up and snuggled with some. One little girl had the most beautiful navy blue eyes, just like Anne's were at birth. Telling Laura their stories and interacting with the nurses and parents allowed her to understand better what I did. She was quite delighted to see the big babies as well as the small ones and wasn't scared to see all the lines and tubes. She mostly took delight in learning their first names and meeting their mothers. In doing this, I felt slightly vindicated, but I still worry that in our efforts to give vent to our frustrations, we had said too much around our children while they were growing up.

Soon after, another remarkable case challenged my attitude about the limits of neonatal intensive care. Intraventricular hemorrhage, or IVH, is one of the worst complications of prematurity. These brain hemorrhages are graded from 1 to 4. Grade 1 IVH is small and rather mild. Grade 2 hemorrhage fills one or both brain ventricles, the cavities that usually hold spinal fluid, with blood. Grade 3 means the blood clots in the brain ventricles obstruct the flow of spinal fluid and cause them to enlarge. Grade 4 IVH, the most severe, occurs when the blood clots spread into the brain tissue itself. Charlie was a small premature infant, born at 23 weeks gestation and 650 grams birth weight, who survived despite bilateral grade 4 brain hemorrhages. There were huge blood clots in his brain injuring significant brain tissue on both sides. If he survived, he would certainly have major neurological deficits.

Charlie's father was a rotund, gregarious evangelical preacher who gratefully appreciated everything we did, and he prayed for miracles. He typically spoke on behalf of his wife, and he continually thanked the bedside nurses for their care. Halfway into his NICU stay, Charlie developed a fungal, or yeast, bloodstream infection. His central venous line had allowed access of a common fungus into his body, so we began IV antifungal medication. Unfortunately, he also developed hydrocephalus, or obstruction of the flow of cerebrospinal fluid within the brain. In assessing his hydrocephalus, we discovered that there was yeast growing in his spinal fluid as well. Both the bilateral grade 4 IVH and the fungal meningitis meant that, if he survived, he would be profoundly impaired.

One quiet afternoon when his parents were sitting at his bedside, I discussed his extreme prematurity, severe brain bleeds, meningitis, and most likely outcomes with Charlie's parents. I mentioned to them that this was an appropriate time to consider offering him no further aggressive interventions, but to offer him comfort care instead. The father's body language abruptly changed, he sat upright and strongly disagreed. I respected his view but felt that he did not really comprehend his son's potential, so I called in an experienced and respected pediatric neurosurgeon for consultation. After examining the baby and all his studies, the neurosurgeon also sat with the parents, reviewed his findings, and told them that he recommended they do nothing and allow him to die of his complications of prematurity. The father disagreed with his opinion as well. And then, the next day, he surprised us all by asking to have another neonatologist assigned to care for Charlie. That meant, essentially, that he was firing me. Having never been fired by parents before, I was startled but gladly agreed to let one of my younger, more passive partners take over his care. On one level, I understood that Charlie's dad wanted to direct his son's care, but on another level, I disagreed with him.

The substitute neonatologist called in a different neurosurgeon who proceeded to place a ventriculo-peritoneal shunt, or VP shunt, to drain the obstructed spinal fluid from Charlie's brain into his abdomen. Unbelievably, that baby survived and went home after several more months of intensive care. Two years later the father brought Charlie back to the NICU to see everyone. His son was in a stroller, profoundly impaired with cerebral palsy and seizures, could not see, was fed by a tube, and could not communicate. I still believe that this baby would have been better off dying from all his horrible injuries. Perhaps I did not counsel these parents correctly, or I revealed too much of my own feelings about quality of life. Perhaps this father had some other reason to want his son alive at all costs. Charlie's outcome was extremely disheartening to me, and his case illustrates the fact that NICU care often goes too far and does too much—just because we can. NICU care sometimes offers false hope, and clearly it produces children who will never know anything that resembles an ordinary life.

A third exceptional case illustrates parental suffering and the futility of NICU care. Sophia was a precious, full-term baby girl whose reserved, Muslim mother noticed that she stopped moving in utero two days before her birth. This was her mother's first pregnancy, and everything had been normal until then. The mother went to see her obstetrician, reported decreased fetal movement, and her OB performed a non-stress test in the office. This test shows fetal movement and heart rate variability. Healthy babies respond with increased heart rate during movement, however this test showed Sophia to be nonreactive, or abnormal. Her mother was sent to the hospital for a contraction stress test. This test likewise showed her baby to be in trouble. Then an emergency C-section was performed. Sophia did not move or breathe when she was born, but her heart rate was around 100 and she was easy to resuscitate. A tube was inserted into her trachea, and as ventilation began, her heart rate and color improved. Still, she did not move. She was taken to the NICU, where she was supported on a ventilator. Unfortunately, Sophia remained limp and essentially nonresponsive.

During the next two days, many tests were performed to assess the severity of the brain injury that Sophia had suffered, presumably from lack of oxygen (hypoxia) and low blood flow in utero. Her electroencephalogram, or EEG, was nearly flat. Her brain scan showed no brain hemorrhage but was suspicious for hypoxic injury—low oxygen. The magnetic resonance imaging of her brain — an MRI exam—showed significant early brain injury. Sophia did not wake up, move, or respond to pinprick stimuli. She had no suck or swallow. Of course, she was given IV nutritional support and appropriate medications. A pediatric neurologist was consulted, and more laboratory tests were done to rule out other causes of coma in a newborn.

Sophia developed acute renal failure (kidney injury from low oxygen in utero) and did not urinate for eight days. Her kidney function recovered by ten days of age. However, another EEG at that time was unchanged, nearly flat. Her MRI then revealed definitive global brain injury from low oxygen. Her neurologic exam was unchanged. Her parents were struggling to cope with the evolving evidence that Sophia's brain had been severely injured in utero. There were many discussions with these parents about the status of their daughter's brain injury and the slim potential for improvement. She was not brain-dead, but she was very close, since only her brain stem functioned clinically.

On several occasions, her parents expressed their strong Islamic faith and wished to continue her intensive support. We all felt miserable for them because there was nothing more that we could do but wait. The baby tolerated tube feedings of her mother's breast milk. Every day when she visited, this young mother, wearing her headscarf and sitting for long hours next to her bed, cried quietly and expressed her guilt at not knowing what to do when her baby stopped moving. Sophia's father remained solemn and pensive, yet supportive of his wife. He was appreciative of all the information they were given. After two weeks of Sophia's lack of movement and lack of response to stimuli, her parents were told that it would be appropriate to take her off the ventilator. They agreed, and this was planned for the next evening. I carefully removed her endotracheal tube, and as I sat there with her parents at the bedside, she started breathing on her own. We had not expected that. Her blood pressure and oxygen levels remained quite stable, in fact. Even though she continued to breathe, her neurologic exam did not change. That evening, her mother quietly cried but declined to hold her. We continued her feedings and watched and waited. Nothing changed clinically with this beautiful baby girl for another week. Then her parents came in one morning when she was three weeks old and asked for her feedings to be stopped. This faithful couple decided that her soul had left her body and that she was essentially dead already. They explained to me that this was their strong religious belief.

Since she was clearly not brain-dead, there were nurses in our Catholic hospital who objected to this approach. I wanted to grant the parents' wishes and withhold her feedings, which would allow their daughter to die peacefully in our NICU. Some of the other doctors and nurses agreed with the parents' request, but the hospital nursing administrator and legal counsel would not allow this. So, the NICU social worker helped me arrange this baby's transfer to the Austin Hospice Christopher House, where she would be cared for during her final days. Once she was transferred there, her tube feedings were discontinued, and four days later, she died peacefully in her mother's arms.

I still believe that this baby need not have been transferred to another facility in order to allow her parents to let her go. I think that moving her merely added to her parents' suffering, given all that they had already been through. I was unhappy and disheartened with how the hospital system treated these parents of a different faith and religious beliefs. In my view, the medical system did not lessen their burden as they coped with their daughter's brain damage. In the end, the system contributed to their suffering.

Finally, there was Sally. To me, she was the most striking case I ever encountered that illustrated medical futility in the NICU. She was born at full term to a female soldier stationed at a base in Texas. At birth, Sally was discovered to have a cloacal exstrophy. Her urinary bladder, vagina, and rectum came together into a cloacal pouch that emptied onto the outside of her abdomen. Her abdominal wall muscles, skin and bones did not form. Her kidneys were both malformed, one very small and the other large and obstructed (it would not drain urine). She had no uterus. She was transferred to Dell Children's Hospital NICU, where various surgical subspecialists evaluated her. The pediatric urologist created a ureterostomy, a ureteral opening, to the outside of her abdomen for drainage of urine from the better kidney. The pediatric surgeon created a colostomy, or colonic opening, to the outside of her abdomen for drainage of stool. Sally was born with an anatomic anomaly of extreme proportions.

The surgical teams adeptly created bypasses for her defects as best they could; these were not technically fixes, though. The medical team disagreed about the best approach for her care. Her first urinary tract infection was easy enough to treat. Some argued that she could be cared for at home by her father, while her mother was away on active duty. However, her father departed from their lives when she was about six months old. After a few months, Sally's abnormal kidneys began to fail, and she needed dialysis, even though she would never be a candidate for a kidney transplant. There was no room to insert a donor kidney into her very abnormal abdominal cavity. Some of us, including her nephrologist (my husband), thought that dialysis was futile and that we should counsel the mother to let her go. Others thought that dialysis would offer her some quality of life appropriate for a baby.

So, Sally grew up in our NICU on peritoneal dialysis. She needed a gastrostomy tube for special formula administration since she sucked poorly. She experienced many other complications, but the nurses loved her, nonetheless. They dressed her in charming pink and yellow outfits and fixed her short brown hair with matching bows. She was a cute baby. They decorated her room with banners and balloons, and the child life specialist "played" with her every day. About ten months of age she developed blindness, for no discernable reason, and she had other neurological delays as well. Sally continued to be an easy baby as far as her temperament went. She tolerated visitors and enjoyed being rocked and listening to her music. She remained calm and happy while cruising the unit in her wagon and could hear people saying hello to her. She learned to sit in her highchair and eat a few mushy foods. She tolerated all the fuss for her one-year birthday celebration held in the NICU, and it seemed as if she almost smiled for some of the pictures.

The nephrologist kept telling the mom that Sally's dialysis could be thought of as futile therapy, but some of the neonatologists persisted in their disagreement. They told the mom to press on. So, at sixteen months of age, Sally went home from the NICU on peritoneal dialysis, and the procedure was performed at home by her mother. A fluid cycling machine kept the fluids going into and out of her abdominal cavity. Mom had been trained to work the dialysis cycler and change out the fluids. Sally was readmitted once for a peritoneal infection, which was treated, and she returned home again. When Sally was twenty-six months old, her young mother finally asked the nephrologist if she could "quit doing all of this." He told her, "Yes, of course; this treatment is totally up to you since you are the one who has to do it." Then he wrote orders to stop dialysis. A few days later, Sally died peacefully at home.

What was the point of all that baby girl had gone through? We knew from the start that she could not be completely corrected or transplanted. In retrospect, I think that some of the nurses and doctors were just too much in love with her to let her go. Did she have a comfortable life? Maybe, but to what end? Had this been the best thing for her entire family? Her parents were divorced. I have no idea how her big brother at home was faring as a result of all her hospitalizations and his mother's absences. Did we do all of this just because we could, or for her wellbeing? And just where was that dividing line in cases like little Sally's?

These challenging cases illustrate how the concept of futile care can be controversial and sometimes difficult to define. In the past, efforts to prolong a baby's life in the NICU were once considered part of the healing process, but NICU care today may inadvertently prolong dying or suffering. When an infant's death is delayed at the price of suffering, or when survival is associated with severe disabilities and an unbearable life for the child and his or her parents, the use of every treatment available in the NICU may be considered inappropriate. My exceptional cases demonstrate that setting limits to neonatal intensive care because of a baby's incurable condition or an extremely poor neurological prognosis is neither simple nor straightforward. Fortunately, neonatal palliative care (also known as comfort, or hospice, care) can be provided as a more humane way to help parents and staff work through the agonizing process of coping with the apparent futility of NICU care.

Chapter 17

BURNOUT

All working mothers know that three children are tougher to handle than two. Another axiom that was unknown to me in my early years is that mothering never ends, at least not until you get them through the teenage years, off to college, and well into young adulthood. Traveling for AAP and ABM, teaching at various national conferences, were welcome intellectual distractions, although in the meantime, both of my girls were developing anxiety disorders. I had much to learn about these mental maladies, and I discovered that they were common—more than twenty percent of American females have an anxiety disorder. In addition, Laura began to show signs of a mood disorder that required specialized treatment. After years of unending maternal love, patience, and understanding, during that period of turmoil with Laura's awful teenage behavior, I suffered maternal burnout. Previously, I had been able to compartmentalize my two worlds—medicine and motherhood—but now they were colliding. I was glad when Laura went off to college.

At this same time, I was still taking call in the hospital at night, and with all the typical obligations of my practice—attending deliveries, meeting prenatally with parents, counseling mothers in preterm labor, and supervising NNPs—I was growing weary. Oh, how I wished our practice had an age cutoff for taking night call in the hospital. At age sixty-two, I felt old, and then I experienced one final bad evaluation.

"Lacks compassion" was the comment that slapped me in the face. It was written by a younger, reserved, yet affable partner when he evaluated me one last time. We were all accustomed to annual peer evaluations, but this time I was shocked and extremely hurt. I had practiced medicine for thirty-three years and never heard any such comment made about me. How had I arrived in a position in which anyone might say such an awful thing about a seasoned neonatologist? Yet, part of me understood where this man's feelings originated. His feedback resulted from our sharing the care of one particular premature baby, a tiny baby born at 23 weeks gestation, weighing only 650 grams—the tiny preemie who managed to survive on a ventilator despite huge, bilateral brain hemorrhages, fungal meningitis, and hydrocephalus. If he survived, these devastating complications would guarantee him a profoundly abnormal neurodevelopmental outcome. After describing this likely outcome to his parents, I recommended that we provide no additional intensive care or treatments, that we offer him comfort care instead. When his father requested another neonatologist be assigned to care for his son, I relinquished the baby's care to my partner, the one who later issued that caustic evaluation.

Around that time, I caught myself making rounds with the nurses in the NICU and pessimistically discussing a perfectly normal, thriving preterm baby, a so-called "feeder-grower." He was outgrowing his apnea (breathing pauses), learning to feed well, and gaining weight. Nevertheless, I sighed loudly, turned, and reported, "This is a perfectly normal preemie; something is bound to go wrong." They all chuckled, but I was serious. After I turned sixty, I noticed that my interest in work was beginning to wane. I avoided meetings, and no new projects interested me. I began to dread upcoming call nights. When I was on call, I stayed holed up in my call room reading whenever possible. The new hospital electronic medical record was frustratingly cumbersome and slow, and it gave me small pleasure that I would not have to bear it much longer.

I began to realize that I lost not only my energy but also my enthusiasm. I mumbled to myself "Oh, bother" while hurrying to yet another high-risk delivery.

I grew weary of seeing bad things happen to little babies. I had been practicing neonatology for so long that I was feeling discouraged and disinterested. Then I noticed myself becoming more cynical and irritable. Some days I didn't care very much at all what happened. Once, when I was asked to attend the delivery of a 27 weeks gestation premature baby, I groaned to my co-worker, "Oh, dear, here comes another one," but then I caught myself. What was I saying? This was somebody's beloved baby about to be born. My extreme negativity made it clear that I was burning out.

I felt so continually overloaded with NICU work and chronic stress that I poured myself a glass of wine when I came home every night. Drinking away the stress didn't accomplish much. In earlier years, I had been able to decompress from the day by talking with my colleagues or my husband. Toward the end of my career, however, even that didn't help, and my practice of neonatology began to feel like a struggle. I had stood by too many premature infants while their parents and I watched them breathe their last breaths. I had helped too many families decide the right time to remove their babies from ventilators and allow them to die of their disease. I had counseled too many mothers facing imminent delivery of an extremely preterm baby at 24- or 25-weeks gestation.

After thirty-three years, I was fried from practicing neonatology—drained dry by complicated cases, life-threatening birth defects, and needy parents. What I did not realize until late in my career was the effect of all those challenges, all those long hours, and all that stress. When I finally began to recognize burnout, it occurred to me only then that it had all been too much. During those final months of awareness, the worst part was feeling that I no longer made a difference.

Burnout is characterized by emotional exhaustion, depersonalization, and diminished feelings of personal accomplishment. For physicians, it is the result of work-related stress and long hours. Unlike major depressive disorder, which pervades all aspects of a patient's life, burnout is a distinctly work-related syndrome. The loss of emotional, mental, and physical energy is due to continued job-related demands, especially taking night call. Depersonalization is a sense of emotional distance from your patients or your job. And finally, feelings of low personal accomplishment give you a decreased sense of self-worth or purpose.

Ultimately, I arrived at the point at which I did not want to visit with expectant parents whose baby would be born with a severe birth defect. I used to appreciate having those prenatal visits with parents. They were opportunities for kind explanations, patient answers, and hope. I once thrilled at taking care of extremely ill newborn infants and premature babies. I enjoyed watching them get well. I once had great compassion, enough to take care of hundreds of babies, enough to hold their mothers' hands, and enough to answer all their parents' questions. I showed empathy when I gave all my effort to stabilize a baby, provide the best care, or give parents a reassuring update. I felt great compassion as I sat with parents during their newborn baby's untimely death.

I have followed with interest recent Facebook postings in the Physician Moms Group. These young female physicians share problems that they confront with their children, their spouses, and their work. Lately, I have been struck by all the discussions about burnout. Most physician moms mention a health care system that asks too much of them, too many patients seen in too little time, long work shifts, productivity quotas, patient satisfaction surveys, and the like. Of course, the electronic medical record is the biggest villain, not to mention office and hospital administrators who are blatantly unsympathetic.

Nurses tell them that they lack compassion; patients say they are critical. These young physician moms describe feeling like they are supposed to be doing more—more patients, more charting, more time to listen. They feel as if they are supposed to be giving more—to their patients, to their spouses, to their families. Furthermore, they feel that doing more and giving more works for everyone but them. One physician aptly described her situation as "compassion fatigue." From my perspective, they are all describing situations in which they continually respond to the needs of others but cannot take the time needed to care for themselves.

From postings about their children's issues, these female physicians seem to be relatively early in their careers. Most are probably in their thirties and forties. I remember feeling tired during those years, sometimes exhausted, but not burnt out. I remember feeling disappointed or angry during those years, but not burnt out. I was not stronger or tougher than they are. I was not better at coping with the demands of a medical practice. I did not have more resilience than they do.

The current health care system is affecting their lives negatively sooner than it affected mine, and this is a worrisome trend.

I do not pretend to have the solution for these physician mothers' burdensome situations. But I can look back and recall what kept me sane in my early years. Regular exercise and time with friends were paramount. Playing with my children was extremely worthwhile, as was doing anything enjoyable to fill up my cup. Engaging in mindless needlework somehow became a meditative practice. Venting to others at work, about work, always helped. Call it whining or b****ing; it still helped. Talking with a professional, a psychiatrist or psychologist, to unpack the issues in play, was invariably helpful. Identifying which plates to take down is necessary.

Flexible work schedules, part-time or reduced hours may be the only solution for some. It was for me, at one time or another. Job-sharing arrangements may have to be created. Reasonable shift lengths, with days off, and sufficient staffing are crucial. Choosing not to go into work when you are ill is especially important; any decent job must provide paid sick days. Some claim that meditation and practicing yoga help, but I never used these tools successfully. The two best pieces of advice that I received along the way were "Take down some plates" and "Learn to say no." One young physician mom summed it up perfectly: "Lean out."

A couples' support group, like our Healing the Healer group in Houston, might provide adequate structure and the correct format to discuss how the practice of medicine invades one's life. Our intergenerational group unexpectedly provided both understanding and solutions. My husband and I were well into the three-year life span of our group when we began to feel the love, acknowledgment, and support of the other healers. It takes a while to get to know each other, to dig below the surface, and to let down your defenses.

I was much older than these younger moms when my work began to burn me out and discourage me. At the time of my burnout, I was experiencing another sort of overwhelming problem in my personal life. My youngest child, Laura, had developed a severe anxiety disorder, and as a result of excessive drug use, her attempt to self-medicate, she flunked out of college in her senior year. When she was not hysterically screaming at me, she accused me of lacking compassion.

There it was again: lacks compassion. By then, I had spent my entire adult life caring for others—my patients, their parents, and my own children.

So, I found myself at age sixty-two, not only fried but also presented with an opportunity to work part time, an easy thirty-five hours a week. Our practice needed a physician to care for babies in an intermediate care nursery and to attend normal deliveries at a small outlying hospital. For me, this change became a blessing. That final switch in practice—from the NICU to the normal newborn nursery—for those last two years of my career was a lifesaver. It also provided me with a happy ending to my long career in neonatology.

Chapter 18

RELIEF

I t came as unexpected grace—an opportunity to work part time in a low-risk delivery hospital and care for newborns who didn't need intensive care. This work was nothing like the NICU, and it was a lifesaver. Volunteering to help these newborns and supervise a small intermediate care unit was an easy decision. Our practice contracted with this smaller hospital to provide delivery coverage, and no one else wanted to take care of newborns who didn't have health conditions. All my partners thought it would be boring. Boring sounded pretty good to me.

During a meeting to decide who would cover this nursery, the issue of my age came up, and one of my younger partners turned to me and asked, "Are you really sixty-two?" When I nodded, he looked surprised and told me that his mother was sixty-two. So, I took the job covering normal deliveries and caring for newborns. It required me to work a few days each week and cover some weekend nights. This was the perfect part-time position, just enough hours (about thirty) to maintain my health insurance benefits and retirement plan savings.

I enjoyed more regular exercise, joined a hand-bell choir at church, and started piano lessons. I taught myself calligraphy, a superb hobby for a perfectionist. I enjoyed lunches with friends while working part time for the last two years of my career. Among the newborns I cared for were several interesting and not-so-normal cases, as well as circumcisions gone awry. Then there was one last remarkable code of a baby delivered footling breech whose head was stuck in his mother's vagina.

The work was effortless, and I quickly discovered that it was uplifting to be there. Mostly, I examined newborn babies or attended deliveries all day. A nice group of OBs, all women, did a fine job of delivering mothers with normal pregnancies—there were no high-risk patients. I discovered how wonderful it was to see babies who were completely healthy, well-grown, and normally responsive. The new mothers asked ordinary questions about baby care, breastfeeding, pacifiers, and vaccinations. The dads were all interested in circumcisions. Toddler and school-age siblings with pink or blue balloons came to visit, and proud, happy grandparents were everywhere. It was a joyful place to work. The L&D nursing staff was superb and, once again, on the unit we felt a sense of camaraderie. Moreover, the staff was supportive of breastfeeding and appreciated my expertise and comfort level with that clinical challenge.

I relished holding and snuggling with newborn babies after examining them in their mother's room. Rarely did I wake a sleeping baby and, to make a point, I never interrupted breastfeeding. Demonstrating how babies loved to be swaddled and taking the time to teach parents how to do this was satisfying. I showed them exactly how babies quiet down when you cuddle them, hold them tightly swaddled, and sway back and forth. I taught the five S's: sucking, swaddling, swaying, shushing, and side or stomach lying. Many new parents had seen the video "*The Happiest Baby on the Block*,"[17] which describes these five S's. This prompted great discussions about the use of pacifiers and how they may or may not interfere with breastfeeding.

In fact, newborn babies really do love to suck. They suck not only for hunger, but also for comfort. I taught parents about hunger cues, the ways in which a newborn lets mom know that she is ready to nurse. New mothers and fathers were surprisingly unaware of newborn hunger cues. Everyone knew about crying, but crying is a late sign of hunger. I enjoyed talking about breastfeeding

---

17 *Happiest Baby on the Block*; https://www.happiestbaby.com

and demonstrating the five S's to new parents with healthy newborn infants. It was such a nice change of pace. Holding and snuggling normal newborns proved to be therapeutic, and I remembered how much I loved babies.

There was the occasional baby with a low blood sugar who required an IV, a baby with a low temperature who needed evaluation for possible infection, a baby who had to be observed for possible seizures. During my time there, we experienced only one baby who was dropped on his head by his mother. Mom was sedated at the time, and her mother, the baby's grandmother, was told not to leave Mom alone with the baby. Unfortunately, she did, and soon thereafter, the mother dropped her baby. Everyone was terrified. Thankfully, though, brain imaging showed that no hemorrhage or fractures had occurred.

There was one interesting case of bleeding after a circumcision. The procedure had gone perfectly. Because of some oozing, I held pressure for over an hour, far longer than was usually needed. I applied Surgicel, an absorbable hemostatic wrap, which in most cases stops all bleeding. Worried that the baby might have a bleeding disorder, I sent his blood for clotting factor studies. These quickly returned within the normal range, and I went to inform the parents. In the room with the baby's parents was his grandmother, who told me that her son, the baby's father, had a circumcision at age two, and his penis had bled a lot, too. The father didn't know about this, and it turned out that both the baby and his father had Von Willebrand's disease, a genetic disorder caused by a missing clotting protein. The condition is not as severe as hemophilia, but can show up after circumcision, dental procedures, or with menstruation in girls. The rule illustrated here was: Family history is always important.

One exceptional young mother presented in labor at term and volunteered that she had been using "occasional opioids" for chronic pain. At birth, her baby was small, only four and a half pounds, and very jittery. This mom denied much opioid use, but the baby's pronounced withdrawal symptoms spoke otherwise. The OB didn't know that her patient, the mother, had been "doctor shopping" to obtain pain meds. Despite how her baby was acting, this mother didn't confess to her drug dependence until we confirmed the problem with positive infant urine, stool, and hair toxicology screens for narcotics. If a mother is using drugs, the baby's urine will be positive for that drug for about one day, stool will be positive for two to five days, and hair will be positive for several weeks. There were opioids in all three infant samples, and some marijuana too, confirming significant maternal drug use and therefore intrauterine exposure to narcotics. The baby's small size was also consistent with maternal opioid abuse. This baby girl developed severe neonatal abstinence syndrome and took many weeks to wean off oral morphine. Her mother was referred to a pain management clinic; I have no idea, however, if she was successfully weaned off narcotics. We sent the baby home with her grandparents.

One larger preterm baby was born at 36 weeks gestation with an unusual skin rash. Her mother had presented with prematurely ruptured membranes one week earlier and remained in the hospital waiting to deliver. The baby delivered vaginally and was quite vigorous. She cried, moved around, and turned pink as expected. Quite unexpectedly, though, she had a scalded skin appearance on a large part of her anterior abdominal wall—her "stomach." I had no idea what this rash was. Of course, the mother and her sisters were curious and asked me many questions. They seemed miffed that I didn't recognize the rash. No one had reportedly been ill with any viral type symptoms. I took pictures of the rash with my iPhone and sent them to my friend, the pediatric dermatologist, but he didn't recognize the rash either.

We placed the baby on antibiotics for possible infection and observed her in the nursery for two days. Infant and mother's blood cultures, for bacteria, all remained sterile. The baby remained clinically stable without symptoms of bacterial infection. Two days later, however, her rash changed. Small vesicles, or blisters, had cropped up around the edges of this large rash. I knew immediately that it must be Herpes Simplex virus. I took some new pictures and sent off viral cultures. We started IV Acyclovir, an anti-viral medication, and after obtaining consent, I performed a spinal tap. Unfortunately, her spinal fluid showed evidence of active viral infection. She had disseminated Herpes Simplex viral infection with meningitis.

I walked into the mother's room to give her the bad news and inform her that we planned to transfer her baby to the Dell Children's NICU for continuing care with the pediatric infectious disease specialists. The mother denied ever having genital Herpes or cold sores on her lips, but she showed me a small scar on her upper chest where there was a blister, "just like a cold sore," two weeks before. It was clear to me then that the baby developed an intrauterine Herpes Simplex infection (explained by the earlier prolonged rupture of membranes). This baby had a reasonable response to antiviral medication but went home with brain imaging evidence of significant brain damage. Time will reveal the extent of her brain injury while she is followed closely for neurodevelopmental progress. However, I heard later that she was doing well at one year of age (when her mother returned to that facility to deliver another baby).

Circumcisions were the most fun, exciting, and daring part of my two-year stint providing normal newborn care. My husband objected to my doing them so late in my career. He had heard about circumcisions going so wrong that the penis was injured, or denuded, and the parents had no recourse but to sue. In the previous thirty-three years, I saw only one case of a botched circumcision. This baby was admitted to TCH with a partially denuded penis infected with Staphylococcus aureus. This was a serious bacterial infection that responded to IV antibiotics, and fortunately, that little boy did not lose his penis. But he could have.

I didn't listen to my husband's concerns about doing circumcisions; in fact, I got so good at doing them that I grew comfortable allowing fathers to come into the procedure room and watch. Oddly enough, most of the dads preferred to watch this procedure if given the chance. The baby boys were gently restrained and sucked on a sucrose pacifier to keep them calm. After injecting lidocaine, a local anesthetic, at the base of their penis, I carefully snipped off their foreskin using a Gomco clamp device. Doing this procedure while the baby was calm and/or sleeping was gratifying. Every now and then we would find a hypospadias, a birth defect in which the urethral opening comes out of the edge of the glans penis, instead of in the middle. These babies needed referral to the pediatric urologist for repair at a later age; their circumcision would have to wait. Every now and then some bleeding would occur after a routine circumcision and I would be tempted to send clotting studies.

Performing circumcisions gave me an opportunity to chat with the fathers and ask them about things—why folks feared vitamin K shots or doubted the benefits and safety of vaccinations. I learned that attitudes against the provision of routine medical care were mostly the result of Internet searches or celebrities' opinions. Parents commonly asked "Dr. Google." To me, this meant that they had looked something up on the Internet without discernment as to whether the site from which they got information was legitimate. By that time, I had grown to hate "Dr. Google" and all his disinformation. I resented the way "Dr. Google" led people to mistrust our well-founded, published, medical advice. I spent a lot of time during my last two years attempting to disprove misinformation and encourage parents to do the right thing.

One case that stands out involved a handsome, muscular father in his late thirties, a retired Navy Seal. He was adamant about not trusting any medical advice that the "government had its hand in." He refused to listen to my explanations of how NIH-funded research findings are the best that exist, usually resulting from well-controlled trials published only after peer reviews to the nth degree. In addition, he doubted anything that came from the Centers for Disease Control, including childhood immunization guidelines. I was astonished at his anti-government attitude—he had, after all, worked for the Navy for many years. Yet he sure wanted that circumcision done on his son.

Near the very end of my career, working in this quiet L&D unit, I had an opportunity to perform another amazing code. A healthy young mother walked into L&D with her baby's little feet hanging out of her vagina. She was pregnant at full term, and her baby was breech. Somehow, she ruptured her membranes and went into labor with the baby's feet presenting first. So, the OB and nursing staff quickly transported the mother with her footling breech presentation back to the operating room for delivery. The worried mom was given an IV sedative while the OB tried desperately to deliver this baby. But his head became wedged in the mother's cervix, her uterine outlet. Fortuitously for me, I stood there waiting with a skilled NICU nurse and a trained NICU respiratory therapist (not usually the case in this quiet intermediated care unit). We had all the necessary equipment ready. This was reassuring, but we all expected a badly depressed baby.

After an excruciating twelve minutes of watching the OB tug on the baby boy's feet and limp legs, this little guy was finally delivered—blue, limp, lifeless, and not breathing. But he had a good heart rate, around 100. We proceeded to resuscitate him, and everything went perfectly. The endotracheal tube went in correctly and was secured well, his ventilation was ideal, the IV insertion was flawless, the meds were administered as they should be, and by five minutes of age his heartbeat was a normal 140 and he became pink. He gasped for a few minutes, then began to breathe regularly and move around, all reassuring signs. At about twenty minutes of age, he looked great, so we removed his breathing tube and took him to see his mom briefly, then brought him to the nursery for observation. I felt certain that he would be fine.

After talking with his terrified parents and reassuring them both, after the nurses took the baby to the nursery for monitoring and lab checks, I walked down the chilly and quiet hospital corridor alone. I felt ecstatic. I felt high and quite wonderful. I realized that I had not felt that way in over a year, since I was last in the busy NICU. It was at that moment that I recognized that I was on an adrenaline high. I suddenly realized how intense epinephrine surges had propelled me throughout my career, always providing energy and a huge sense of accomplishment. It dawned on me that I had spent a good part of my life in the NICU as an epinephrine junkie. I craved excitement and valued being called from one interesting or demanding situation to another. Looking back, my NICU practice had always been thrilling, sometimes even scary. But mostly it had been thrilling.

Chapter 19

GOOD ENOUGH MOTHER

I n my thirties, in Houston, I had intended to be a perfect mother. Full-time work in the NICU, three small children, and unacceptable behavioral habits cemented by my own upbringing proved me otherwise. Later, when I turned forty, the painful move to Arkansas brought out the worst in me. Because I disliked my work there and felt continually stressed, I noticed, at various times, some bad mother forces bubbling up from within. I dearly loved my children, although I remember yelling at them often when I was overwhelmed, or they were out of control. Thank goodness my hitting one of them was rare; that trauma transpired only twice in a decade. My children were wonderful and innocent, and they adapted, for the most part, rather well to our move. Looking back now, I worry that my stress-filled life created a home atmosphere that trickled down into anxiety. At the time, I hoped that my husband's levelheadedness and calm nature would counterbalance my impulsive tendencies sufficiently. Hopefully, it did at times.

Later, while living and raising a family in Austin, there arose another dark period for me. While working full time, often sixty hours a week, I would return home Sunday morning after a strenuous or demanding twenty-four-hour shift on

Saturday. I was tired and grouchy, and I inevitably walked into a messy kitchen, and my shadow-self emerged. I erupted and shrieked, "Why can't someone clean up the kitchen before I get home?" There were dishes from the night before, and my husband had already left for work. Then I would scowl, clean the kitchen myself, and stomp off to get some sleep. After my nap, I would find my children and apologize. They must have thought I was crazy, or at the very least inconsistent. It was extremely tough to control myself both at work and at home. I could keep it together at work—where everything was orchestrated to be under control—only to return home, find things gone haywire, and let loose. Why do we always do or say the worst things to those we love the most?

I have heard some say that motherhood is a marathon, but I disagree. You do not train to be a mother, nor do you pace yourself during your motherhood tenure. I believe that motherhood is more like a decathlon. Some things you do very well, and others, not so much. You need strength, endurance, flexibility, and psychological stamina. Different events require different skills, and competitions are held on different days. It is the total number of points, each event's score added onto the next—the total attention, understanding, and love—deliverable throughout the long haul of the motherhood decathlon that counts.

I like to remember the successes, those individual moments when I clearly won a big event: It was March, and the ocean was aquamarine blue. The four senior high girls were sprawled out on lounge chairs near the shore with several umbrellas plunged into the white sand around them. They were laughing and talking, sipping virgin daquiris and pina coladas. We moms sat together in the shade by the pool eating lunch. For Anne and her three best friends, this was our spring break mother-daughter trip to Playa Del Carmen, a resort on the Yucatan peninsula of Mexico. Each mother-daughter pair slept together in one room, and we enjoyed breakfast and supper all together as a group. Otherwise, the girls were free to do whatever they liked, including visit bars and clubs in the evenings. Thankfully, one of the mothers was a younger, energetic obstetrician who accompanied the girls out every evening—to protect them.

On the last night of our stay, Anne and I were applying makeup in our room. She stood at the mirror, looking tan and gorgeous, and said, "Mom, can you help me get birth control pills?" I asked if she needed them immediately, to which she blushed, and replied, "No, Mom." Then she confided that she was thinking about having sex next year in college and wanted to be prepared. That night, she trusted me enough to discuss that delicate issue and ask for my support, and the love and satisfaction I felt at that moment was incomparable.

The senior scrapbook was another big event for which I undoubtedly racked up big points. This was a labor of love that I created and presented to each child when they turned twenty-one—a collection of their best childhood memories. Having saved every report card, every school certificate, each blue ribbon, all the programs, and every class picture, I was able to spread these items out on the dining room table and happily sort through them. Buying scrapbook materials and clever embellishments at Michael's was so much fun. It was easy to find kits for scouts, summer camp, sport teams, music, and for each school year. The evening that I presented David with his scrapbook, we were sitting in a quiet restaurant in San Antonio. He sat silently, studied, and thumbed each and every page. Then he looked up at me, grinned, and said, "Thanks, Mom. I had no idea you saved it all." And I felt wonderful.

Not at all like her older sister, Laura was free-spirited and quirky in high school. She began professional therapy with an adolescent psychiatrist when she was fourteen and has continued working with her ever since. As a teenager, she showed symptoms of anxiety and had profound mood swings and temper outbursts. She was given medication for anxiety and, later, a mood stabilizer. At that time, I was the wrong mother for her, since most of her explosions were directed at me. For a while, I regressed and fought back. Anne had been so good, and Laura was being so bad. Even when Anne was very ill with her eating disorder, she was always cooperative; Laura never was. I began professional therapy at the same time because presumably everything happening with Laura was somehow my fault. That disgraceful, old speech replayed in my consciousness: I was a bad mother. It took me nearly three years of therapy to learn what was my part in her struggles and what was hers. Anne was away in college by then, and David had advanced on to graduate school.

From the time that Anne developed an eating disorder in high school and later when Laura turned into an impossible teenager, I struggled with the concept of being a good enough mother. I never considered myself to be a good mother when anything went wrong in my children's lives. My default positions were always guilty, inadequate, absent, or angry. I never thought of myself as good enough when I was exhausted from work. And yet I wanted to work as a physician and be a good mother, too. This was my personal and perplexing living contradiction. I thought that I was able to deal with each child when they needed me, and that I was able to accept help from my husband, teachers, and counselors. I always delighted in and cherished all my children's accomplishments, and I saw them as their own, not mine. I was acting merely as their facilitator. They deserved the credit, which I saw as rightfully earned. But their failures—I somehow saw those as mine. Over time I was able to convince myself that I was present and involved enough when they needed me. But each time something went wrong, I had to work harder to prove myself good enough, that I had given enough patience, enough guidance, enough discipline, and enough love.

I have no idea how long it takes other mothers to feel like they are good enough. It took me almost ten years to recognize my limitations and to feel confident in my skills as a mother. It took me eighteen years to discern when to let them struggle and when to intervene. David going off to college was a perfect example. He was a careless, messy teenager, so I was ready for him to fly out of the nest. He had no clue what he wanted to be when he grew up, and we knew of no way to help him decide. He attended Trinity University in San Antonio and somehow stumbled into working at the campus TV station. Working as a cameraman, then producer, then director, and finally station general manager, he earned a communication degree, a clear divergence from our science backgrounds. His summer internship at a large production firm in San Antonio solidified his choice to become a filmmaker, and the next thing we knew, he was accepted to the UCLA graduate school in cinematography, a premiere film school. He found his own calling.

I had an epiphany once, a few years back, during a session with my current therapist. I must have been complaining about my own mother or discussing how I contributed to my young adult children's struggles. She had heard this line of thinking from me many times before. On that particular day though, she asked me, "Are you the way you are because of your mother?" I thought for a few seconds, and countered, "No, of course not." I articulated that I was the way I was because of my life events, my character, my work, and my relationships, not merely my upbringing. Then she calmly spoke to me, "Why do you think that you are the cause of who your children are?"

In retrospect, I wish that I had understood that Anne, while growing up, felt trapped in the middle, typecast as the perfect child. She shared with me recently that since David was wacky and different, and Laura was the baby who acted out, she felt it necessary to behave well and play the calm peacemaker role of the middle child. Such an awful, stressful position I allowed her to claim. I wish I had known how she felt so that I might have encouraged her to shout, act out, get angry, or behave badly in any way the other two did. In her middle child role, she undoubtedly stuffed her feelings and her fears down deeply and attempted to maintain control and peace among us all.

When she was in high school, Anne wrote a paper about women in medicine. She interviewed Dr. Carol Baker, a pediatric infectious diseases expert at Baylor, an old friend of mine. This professor had never married and had no children. She practiced full-time academic medicine, did exquisite research, and published countless, valuable papers. Her whole life was devoted to pediatric medicine. Anne interviewed me, as well, to obtain the perspective of a female physician who was also a mother. In her paper, Anne compared the life of a full-time academic to a physician in private practice, and she discussed the extra demands of having a family. My friend shared with her that she regretted not having children. I told her that I regretted leaving academic medicine. The stark contrast is ironic.

In hindsight, I believe that I unknowingly pushed Anne too much toward medicine. After she finished college summa cum laude, she had a major setback. She struggled with severe anxiety, panic attacks, and developed a major depressive episode. It took her nearly four years to fully recover and to discover what she wanted to do with her life. During this time, she worked as a nanny caring for a Houston couple's three children. Unhappily, I did not see much of my darling Anne during that time. I intentionally kept myself distant to help her individuate and become her own person, at her own pace.

During the early months of her recovery, I was despondent about her illness and her role as a nanny. My NICU work was a welcome distraction, but when I was home alone, I swilled Chardonnay wine, laid on the couch, and repeatedly watched all the Twilight movies. It seemed easier to consider a teenager falling in love with a vampire than my own daughter having to leave medical school. When Anne was willing, and much stronger, she completed nursing school and was selected into a capstone program that offered an internship in pediatric intensive care nursing at TCH. After obtaining her nursing degree, she was offered a job working full time in the PICU at TCH. She found her dream job, a role that made her happy, and one in which she truly excelled. Now she works in the PICU at Dell Children's and has been promoted to nursing supervisor. She loves her PICU patients and fellow providers. Looking back, I am tremendously proud of all the hard work that she accomplished to uncover her own path.

Laura continues to struggle, however. She cannot seem to find her way past the failure of her last year in college. She smokes a lot of marijuana and refuses to admit her addiction. She has trouble holding down a job and paying her bills. Fortunately, she does take advantage of psychiatric help and proper medications, paid for by us. Phillip and I are learning how to set limits with her and stop bailing her out whenever she cries for help. We are learning to stop feeling guilty or sorry for her when she encounters another setback. She is twenty-eight years old, an adult now, and these are her choices. I pray every day that she will learn how to help herself, avail herself of a rehabilitation program, recover, and get well. I know in my heart that she has the capacity to do this.

In the last few years since retirement, I have given tremendous thought to my struggles as a mother while living the paradox of practicing medicine and raising a family. As much as I loved being a physician, as much as those skills made me feel competent, as much as practicing neonatology gave me a sense of importance, I have concluded that I received infinitely more joy in knowing, raising, and loving my children than I ever did from practicing medicine. I am not sorry for having been a practicing physician. Medicine gave me an interesting and wonderful life, but I am most grateful for my life as a mother to three amazing children. They were truly the best gift.

Chapter 20

REFLECTIONS ON PRACTICING MEDICINE

I miss my stethoscope—the small black one with the tiny neonatal head. I wore it around my neck constantly while on duty. It served as an outward symbol of my knowledge and experience. Inwardly, it reminded me of all the things I could detect about a baby by simply looking, listening, and gently touching. You must always listen first, before they start to cry. My little stethoscope was at the ready in any emergency. I used it to reassure nurses of proper endotracheal tube position and adequate breath sounds. I used it to allay a new mother's fears once I determined that her baby's soft heart murmur was innocent.

Over my extensive thirty-five years in practice, I found neonatology to be an intimate specialty. Certainly, it is intimate learning various private things about each baby's parents, but there is a higher intimacy to it. Attending a high-risk delivery and getting to know the parents of a sick baby—from birth until their child, or children, went home—was extraordinary. It allowed me to be a vital part of the child's life during those early weeks and months. I helped him or her get better, get stronger, grow, and thrive. That experience allowed me to share in a singular time in that child's life. You are not part of the family, but you closely witness how the family functions and adapts through an extremely stressful period. In the NICU, you experience with them all their ups and downs.

Those highs and lows were often quite profound. A baby's struggle to survive might be followed by a seemingly miraculous turnaround and healing, or it might just be one long slide off the very edge of the parents' hopes and dreams. And some mothers wanted an answer to the most painful question that exists. While standing at the bedside of her dying baby, a mother would look at me, tears filling her eyes, and ask, "Why would God let this happen?" She wanted to know why God would take away her beautiful baby. I usually paused, then answered as gently as possible that it was not God's will to take her baby or make him die. The disease did that. No loving God would want that for her child. And I told her that sometimes we could not understand God's plan and might not be able to understand it for an exceedingly long time. I would tell her that it might take years to process the meaning of what she was suffering through in losing her baby. Sometimes I would cry, too, and over the years, it became easier for me to cry along with her.

Throughout my medical practice, I rediscovered that every clinical and personal challenge is an opportunity. The hardest lessons are valuable because they inevitably teach you something vital. These lessons are the obstacles that you encounter and overcome along the way, during years of demanding training, during life's transitions, or during the care of your most confounding cases. It still amazes me to think back on all the unique situations and inspiring babies that I encountered. Such a wonderful journey. In my later years, I welcomed being called by younger partners to discuss a problem case or to seek my opinion about a chest X-ray. It felt satisfying, when after decades of seeing such things, there were very few questions that I could not answer.

Along the way, I learned that passion and concern for high-quality care in medicine is honorable. People notice. Parents notice. Emotional commitment to your patients magnifies your talent and ability. In my view, integrity and honesty are constant professional shields. Quality of care is of paramount importance; striving for this, however, takes extra effort. I continue to believe that working collaboratively with other physicians and nurses to provide high-quality care is virtuous.

An important caveat I learned along the way is that perfectionism fits perfectly into medicine, most notably critical care medicine. Grit, overachieving, and self-discipline are powerful predictors of a successful practice. Being a workaholic also lends itself well to a busy medical practice. There is always more work to be done, more calls to be made, more charts to finish, more reading necessary. The brutal truth, however, is that both perfectionism and "workaholism" distract you from your emotions and other important aspects of your life. You end up caring perfectly for others and not caring for yourself.

I believe that education is crucially important in medicine, continuing medical education even more so. Self-mastery throughout the long haul of a medical practice is accomplished by continuous, self-directed learning. Many more than the minimum number of required hours are essential to remain up to date in modern medicine. Academic medical practice is idealistic; however, it is extremely necessary. Only in that setting do young doctors learn how to properly care for patients and seek information. In addition, research pushes medicine forward. Private practice is necessary for providing the bulk of patient care, but it is much more of a chore, personally, and one finishes without a curriculum vitae to disclose your talents and contributions.

In the early months after I retired from my neonatology practice, I felt empty and aimless. After bemoaning these feelings to my friend, a retired psychiatrist, she said to me, "What you are feeling is—being no longer important, no longer needed." That was exactly it. Now I have adjusted to those feelings and look back on my medical practice with love and pride. I cared for thousands of babies and accomplished many good things. I was a skilled, well-respected neonatologist. There is nothing else that I would rather have spent my life doing. However, over the years, I continually worried about being absent so much from my children. Recently, my youngest summed it up kindly. "Yes, you were gone a lot," she said, "but we knew that you were away doing something important."

ADVANCES IN NEONATOLOGY: A HISTORICAL OVERVIEW

1922   Julius Hess described first transport incubator for newborns.

1930   American Academy of Pediatrics was founded.

1938   Charles Chapple designed modern infant incubator (prototype of Isolette).

1938   Robert Gross and John Hubbard successfully ligated a patent ductus arteriosus (PDA), an opening between major blood vessels from the heart.

1943   Alfred Blalock and Helen Taussig performed first "blue baby" operation for Tetralogy of Fallot, a birth defect that affects blood flow through the heart.

1946   Clement A. Smith published *The Physiology of the Newborn Infant*, the first American textbook of neonatology.

1947   Helen Taussig published her landmark textbook, *Congenital Malformations of the Heart.*

1952   Virginia Apgar described a scoring system for assessment of infants at birth, now known as the Apgar Score.

1953   James Watson and Francis Crick uncovered the structure of DNA and published their groundbreaking discovery in the journal *Nature*.

1959   Mary Ellen Avery and Jere Mead discovered surfactant deficiency as the cause of respiratory distress syndrome (RDS).

1960   Alexander Schaffer coined the term neonatology.

1965   Louis Gluck designed the first modern newborn intensive care unit (NICU) at Yale-New Haven Hospital, in New Haven, Conn.

1967   William H. Northway, et al described Bronchopulmonary dysplasia (BDP).

1968   SJ Dudrick published the first report of total parenteral nutrition (TPN) in newborns.

1969   JN Du and TK Oliver described the first use of an open radiant warmer for newborns.

1971   George Gregory described use of continuous positive airway pressure (CPAP) for respiratory distress syndrome (RDS).

1972   Robert Kirby, et al described the first use of Intermittent mandatory ventilation (IMV) for respiratory distress syndrome (RDS) using the BabyBird ventilator.

1973   Marshall Klauss and Avroy Fanaroff published the first edition of *Care of the High-Risk Neonate*.

1975   American Board of Pediatrics began Neonatal-Perinatal Medicine subspecialty certification.

1975   Robert Bartlett published the first use of extra-corporeal membrane oxygenation (ECMO) in infants

1983   American Academy of Pediatrics and American College of Obstetrics and Gynecology published the first edition of *Guidelines in Perinatal Care*.

1984   International Committee for ROP Classification developed the milestone document describing the classification scheme for Retinopathy of Prematurity (ROP).

1987   American Academy of Pediatrics and American Heart Association launched the Neonatal Resuscitation Training Program (NRP).

1990   Food and Drug Administration approved surfactant therapy for RDS.

1996 Centers for Disease Control and Prevention and American Academy of Pediatrics published recommendations for Group B Streptococcus (GBS) screening and antibiotic prophylaxis.

1997 Food and Drug Administration approved use of inhaled nitric oxide for pulmonary hypertension in newborns.

ABOUT THE AUTHOR

Susan Landers, MD, practiced full-time neonatology—the intensive care of critically ill premature and newborn infants—while raising three children. She has worked in academic medicine, on the faculty of two medical schools, and in a private practice. For many years, Susan worked for the American Academy of Pediatrics as an expert in breastfeeding medicine, writing policy, and teaching at national conferences. She has been interviewed by many news outlets about her work using donor human milk in the NICU and her work with the Mother's Milk Bank of Austin. She lives in Austin, Texas.